for

LENNY

with love

and with gratitude

for his joy in music

A Wind from the West

Bernstein and the
New York Philharmonic
Abroad

Books by Evelyn Ames

Only the Loving

My Brother Bird

The Hawk from Heaven
(poems)

Daughter of the House

A Glimpse of Eden

A Wind from the West:
Bernstein and the
New York Philharmonic
Abroad

Frontispiece: *Problems of the world at 35,000 feet.*

A Wind from the West

Bernstein and the New York Philharmonic Abroad

Evelyn Ames

Photographs by Bert Bial, Contrabassoon

Houghton Mifflin Company Boston

1970

First Printing R

Library of Congress
Catalog Card Number: 74–92605

Printed in the United States of America

The author wishes to thank Random House, Inc., for permission to quote portions of "The Pig-Tale" from The Complete Works of Lewis Carroll *(Modern Library Edition).*

Foreword

WHEN WE WERE ABOUT TO LEAVE on tour with the New York Philharmonic, of which my husband Amyas is president, I went out and bought another of the small thick notebooks I like to take with me on a journey and bring home crammed with notes. The passion to record memories and impressions is a curious one. The notes may have no value to anyone else but there is the hope of saving something from the dimming and erasing of time; also, merely by writing about a thing, anything, I find I come into closer relationship with it and know more about it, the way you discover the nature of a summer field by lying right down in the grass.

Keeping a record on this particular journey presented formidable difficulties; the pressure of the schedule was relentless, there were almost no unfilled hours. Still, another kind of pressure kept building up, too — that of the emotions: the joy and wonder of the music, the gratitude for its gift of light and reconciliation in one troubled place after another. Somehow, in fits and starts and with interpolations inside interpolations, a mad jumble of notes did get put down.

It was my friend J. B. Priestley, a great music lover as well as author, who was the first to suggest that traveling with the orchestra would make a good story. But stories, as distinguished from journals, set their own laws — the most exacting one being omission. More has to be left out than can possibly be included, and in this case where almost every day was a variation on the same theme of concerts, travel, crowds of people, and late, late parties, it was imperative to omit a great deal. What is left out of these pages, however, had its own value no less real than what appears and without some of it there would have been no story to write, for, surrounding and sustaining the orchestra and everyone connected with it, was the continuous concern and devotion of many who are not mentioned and were often unknown to us. In every country and city visited, members of our foreign service and people working for Trans World Airlines, beginning with the president and his wife, the Tillinghasts, gave us hospitality, assistance, the most thoughtful kind of consideration. In the fullest meaning of that expression, they cared for us.

Our group filled one jet plane; with the small changes of directors and friends who joined us and left us again, we were fairly consistently a hundred and twenty. Obviously there were musicians whom we came to know quite well and others with whom we did not have the opportunity, though even with these there was the warmth of daily companionship and shared experience. Enjoyed perhaps above all other communication was the exchange of smiles, the little spark of recognition when we discovered one another in strange halls before the concert began: a salutation across the gap separating performers from their audiences.

This book is as much a tribute to them, to an orchestra of extraordinary musicians, as it is to their great director — a tribute to individual virtuosity and musical feeling and to the unity that must be heard to be believed. In Bernstein's own words, they "breathe together." It is also an appreciation of the friendship they extended and which I prize.

All the time we were away, there was someone who should have been with us but who was kept at home by illness — the man who more than any other is the Philharmonic's guardian spirit. This is Carlos Moseley, the orchestra's wholly dedicated and warmly loved managing director. He will never know how much he was missed.

Vienna, May 26, 1969

E. A.

Contents

Illustrations

". . . gilt-filigreed box fronts set with paintings, like old valentines in gold lace." (La Fenice, Venice)

". . . there was a reception afterwards." (Venice)

". . . for the whole orchestra."

Managing.

"And then in midthought, in midpain, we had landed." (Bonn)

"On TV, live . . . bathed in brilliance . . . the music of Berlioz's opium dream."

"While Bernstein autographed for a crowd of two thousand."

". . . a deep sense of gratitude and communion welled up." (Berlin)

A Wind from the West

Bernstein and the

New York Philharmonic

Abroad

I

Overture

On an August afternoon of the "incredible year," 1968, a certain white Boeing 707 was drilling its way over the North Atlantic, away from the low sun that turned it, minute by minute, a deeper gold. Except for its air speed, everything about it was very calm: no turbulence at its altitude of thirty-five thousand feet, a delicate mosaic pavement of cirrus cloud below, and only the barest lifting and settling of its long wings, like the breathing and sighing along of a sailboat on a gentle summer sea.

From the outside (had anyone been there to notice) the plane would have looked as closed up as a house on a winter night. Across both long rows of little windows every shade was tight-drawn, for dinner was over and a movie was being shown. Nothing unusual about any of this except for the passengers, and the cargo. From seat 1A to 20F the cabin was filled with musicians and the belly of the plane with their instruments — trunks and trunks of violins in special padded compartments, huge square trunks with kettledrums and snare drums and suitcases of drumsticks; glistening flutes and horns and trumpets, towering bass viols with their uncurling fern tops in cases taller than a man, and not just one harp but two. (How to pack all that precious cargo tightly and safely had been a gigantic three-dimensional jigsaw puzzle. In order to solve it, scale models and a replica of the cargo space were built, numbered charts drawn as a guide. Even so, and with all the seats in the forward cabin removed, there were too many instruments for one plane; the rest were contained in the body of another eastbound jet also out somewhere over the ocean.)

In the front window seat, across the aisle from the president of the airline and his wife, sat Leonard Bernstein — familiar to who knows how many millions on both sides of the ocean below; beside him his fifteen-year-old daughter, Jamie, and on the aisle Alexander, his thirteen-year-old son. All three were wearing the earphones a stewardess had offered them but only Alexander glanced at the movie from time to time, between filling in the squares of a crossword puzzle. Jamie, her face closed and thoughtful, was writing on sheet after sheet of yellow paper while their father was studying the score of a symphony — Mahler's Fifth, to be exact — the smoke from his cigarette drifting back to us in the seats directly behind.

Felicia, Bernstein's wife, had stayed home in Connecticut with Nina, who was only six, to do what more she could to help get McCarthy nominated in the approaching Democratic Convention. She had already campaigned for him in Wisconsin and Oregon and California (Bernstein himself had addressed monster rallies in the Boston Garden and Madison Square Garden); now she would do whatever was still possible from home. Earlier in the year, too, she had had to be away for several weeks when she had acted one of the principal roles in a revival of Lillian Hellman's *The Little Foxes.* Felicia is a kind of hummingbird being: tiny, vibrant, elusive. Her passionate concern for causes, like her intelligence and her beauty, blazes out, incandescent, then suddenly she has darted away out of the public glare and made herself invisible — is at home, there quietly to relish domesticity, a few close friends, hours of painting. She had been on tour, working her heart out; this one would have to do without her.

Plans for it had been in the active stage for a full year and another year before that in the making. At one time it was thought the orchestra would go "down under" to Australia and New Zealand and, even after Europe and Israel were decided on instead, endless talks and correspondence took place before the nine major European and Near East festivals, which had unanimously made the New York Philharmonic with Bernstein their first choice, were accommodated (or turned down) and the complex itinerary worked out. The sponsorship, too, had been uncertain at first. Then the State Department and Trans World Airlines both came forward to make it possible.

I cannot remember just when Amyas and I thought of going along, but I think it was about a year earlier. We had been in Japan at the same time as the orchestra and attended several concerts, so we knew how rewarding it could be to hear them in foreign places. We were also deeply interested in hearing music in different concert halls, for ever since its opening in the fall of 1962, Philharmonic Hall, the orchestra's home, had been bedeviled with acoustical faults and puzzles and was due in a year's time to undergo what was fervently hoped would be the final corrections. Concert halls and how they sounded were very much on our minds.

But now, on the flight, there were moments when both of us wondered what we were doing on this plane or why we had ever decided to come. Here we were, going off on a tour with an orchestra for five weeks, committed to a schedule of travel and concerts which covered six pages of a closely printed folder and to another schedule of receptions and formal occasions which took up another five typewritten pages. Sample days would involve early morning departures for airports, a flight (usually to another country), often a late afternoon function, then a concert and — invariably — after every concert a reception and supper. Our luggage contained clothes for climates ranging from that of Israel to Denmark and a life that would include parties at embassies and country walks. Two experienced friends, familiar with the musical centers of Europe and with going on such a tour, had given me advice that I would have daily reason to remember. One had reminded me that we were cultural ambassadors and must always look our best; the other had simply burst out with the admonition to have *comfortable shoes,* for which I was to be grateful wherever we went, on Belgian cobbles and in Arab bazaars, in Venetian *viali* and midnight receiving lines — over all the miles we were to cover in jets and cars and boats and everywhere on our own feet as well, since we both love to walk. (It is a funny thing with shoes: as I unpack them at the end of any journey they fill me with unabashed sentiment, even awe. Those dried bits of grass stuck to a sole, that pungent, dusty smell, or just the look of heels and creases in the uppers carry the same magic as ships seen lying at their piers: they have *been there;* they are more convincing than any picture or souvenir.)

This journey, however, was to leave behind a unique testimony to its reality: music. If it weren't for the music, listened to almost every night, I might settle for the whole experience being one of those immensely involved, long-drawn-out dreams you have toward morning, in which you go through a series of dissimilar yet related adventures, always driving on — on toward some conclusion which the first sounds of morning or your need to get up keep you from reaching. But the music, there's no explaining *that* away. I am someone with a very average musical ear who once played the piano moderately well, but I have to hear a melody many times before I can hum it and am terrible at identifying by name compositions I know perfectly well. Yet now whole long sections of Mahler's Fifth Symphony, brilliant phrases and rhythms and passages of Berlioz's *Fantastique,* and other-world fanfares of Harris come and go in my head, almost as though I had dreamed them up myself out of some unknown treasure cave of the unconscious. I see a thousand scenes inside my head; they are there too, but memories of the music feel more intimate, more physical and at the same time more mysterious — an incredible kind of transfusion I received.

And more than music remains: something beyond even Mahler and Haydn, Berlioz and Rossini, Harris and Schuman, superbly as these were played. For, just as we heard them over and over, in the greatest possible variety of settings, so we kept experiencing a meeting of the same opposites — everywhere the conflict of nations and the concert of art; the tearing apart of hate and dissension, the connecting and healing of music till, by the journey's end, we were to be given a binocular vision, as it were, not only of that part of the earth we covered but even of the nature of Life — of Shiva's cosmic dance, holding in one hand the drum that calls forth creation, brandishing in the other the flame-tip of destruction. "I will drum the drum of the Immortal in this dark world!" vowed Siddhartha Gautama, the Buddha. Sometimes it felt as though this was what the whole tour was about.

All that day of crossing the ocean, which began with going out into our Long Island garden soon after sunup to pick roses, flashing globes of dew on petals which glittered with an almost artificial sparkle, and which ended in a high-ceilinged hotel room in Brussels — all that day was a confused cross-rip of excitement, anxiety, anticipation, and something unidentifiable and quite ominous as well. There was also outright horror. This was August twenty-second, the Russians had invaded Prague thirty-six hours before. Bernstein, who feels world events more poignantly than many of us feel things in our own families, was very depressed. When he arrived at Kennedy airport and I greeted him warmly and happily — for we are old and good friends — he said, more sharply than I had ever heard him, "What are *you* so cheerful about?" Well, I felt not at all as cheerful as I must have appeared. A great many unknowns and misgivings were in the air that day as well as general sorrow, and all of us, I would guess, had wrenched ourselves more or less painfully out of home and families and ongoing lives to climb into that jet and fly out into the storm clouds over Europe and Israel. We were leaving behind some terrible thunderheads over our own country, too: June sixth and Robert Kennedy's murder were still cruelly recent, though at home and in familiar settings it is perhaps a little easier, however illusory, to feel sheltered. Also, Amyas and I had just come from six peaceful sequestered weeks on the island of Martha's Vineyard (where we and the Bernsteins first met), whereas "Lenny" was exhausted, having spent every waking minute since finishing the conducting season on the score of a new musical play, never getting enough sleep. He never sleeps enough. "What I'd give anything to have had," he said on the plane, "is a month more for the show, another week to study this score, and a week's vacation. I haven't had any vacation since four days in March." He looked dreadful too, as he sometimes can. I felt for him yet, as so often and demoniacally happens in such a situation, anything I chose to say turned out to be the wrong thing or came out wrong — like a fairy story I dimly remember where frogs instead of speech jumped out of someone's mouth. After studying the Mahler from right after takeoff, he did sleep for a while. All three in front of us slept — Alexander with his head in Jamie's lap, Jamie folded up against her father, the threesome wound into a comforting endless knot of warmth and affection.

Behind us, the plane buzzed with activity, joking, and laughing. Spirits were high and stewards repeatedly had to ask that the aisles be cleared so that they could get through. In several seats near ours, however, the managers were working away as on flights they invariably would be — spreading out on the small shelves in front of them the contents of their bulging briefcases, their work burden increased by the last-minute illness and dropping-out of our managing director, Carlos Moseley. Much of his work was taken over by William Weissel, of an old and titled Austrian family. Lean, trim, and with a kind of eighteenth-century elegance galvanized with a thoroughly twentieth-century drive and efficiency, he had a fierce attachment to his work and to protecting Bernstein, which he did with devoted loyalty. About five feet eight himself, he worked with two other assistant managers, who were dark-haired young lions of formidable size: six-feet-four-inch Nick Webster, in charge of all logistics, and Ken Haas, six feet seven. Nick, with a capacity for work that matched his frame, seemed imperturbable. Both beds of a hotel room white with paper, the telephone constantly ringing, he moved through oceans of detail with scarcely a bow wave, leaving almost no wake. When I asked him once what Ken did, for I had seen him backstage at Philharmonic Hall without clearly knowing his function, he replied, "He's in charge of things that come up." With one hundred and twenty souls, traveling ten thousand miles, there would be plenty to keep him busy, though he, like Nick, was someone who never seemed to lose his cool. Frank Milburn was our press director, and not at all what you might expect him to be. Sophisticated in the ways of the press, he maintained — except on one outstanding occasion — a quiet, unhurried presence and gentleness of manner that refused to be stampeded by any deadlines or pressures. A knowledgeable and experienced musician as well, his judgment was steady and invaluable. These four unusually likable men ran a complex operation superbly.

While all this quiet work proceeded, the aisle of the plane was alive and crowded with traffic, sociable as a street in Venice on Saturday evening. I studied the faces of the musicians who came past, trying to remember names. Although I had met them all at one time or another and knew a few of them, I wanted to try to recognize each man or woman (of which there were four) not just by name but also by the instrument he played. The photographs Willie had given me were beside me in my carryall — pictures of each section, taken during a performance, and single portraits of the first-desk men. For several weeks I had repeated their names at odd moments, reviewing the first violins, then the seconds and violas, the cellos and basses. These last were the easiest; violinists' faces nestled to one side look very different from the way they do when the men are not playing, and just try to make recognizable a blowing woodwind player or the face at the other end of an extended trombone, a coiled-up horn!

Once we were imprisoned behind trays and stemmed wineglasses and plugged into the plane's music programs, things settled down. When Lenny removed his earphones, I asked which program he was listening to. "Mine," he replied. It was the New York Philharmonic, Leonard Bernstein conducting, playing Mahler's Fourth Symphony.

Meanwhile I was watching the film intermittently and with annoyance. There it was, barely ten feet away; we had heard it was very funny, yet one rebels at being that seduced into watching a film, no matter how good. And perhaps when you sit inside a safety belt, with shades drawn down, and any getting up and moving around is made difficult, deep-buried memories of enforced schoolroom attention twitch at some inner nerve of consciousness. At the same time I despise my lack of will for not turning on the overhead light and consistently attending to my own business as the three in front of us were doing, or mostly so: Jamie's head, whenever I saw it, bent over her yellow pad as she wrote and wrote (what?), and Alexander systematically completing his puzzle.

Somewhere in all this came a very strange moment. On the screen there was an astonishingly lifelike scene of a girlie show in New York — one of those probably fortuitous sequences which happen to capture reality so completely that high comedy, tragedy, absurdity, and dignity are all whirled in a centrifuge together — while in front of me Lenny was hearing himself conduct (back in New York) a hundred and six musicians now seated behind him. Then he raised the shade at his window on a view of sunset-radiant clouds piled high above the Atlantic, their silent passing presences indicating that no-where in which we all were or, rather, had been a moment before: a continually six-hundred-mile-an-hour changing no-where; a dreamlike at-onceness of sight and sound and experience with no separation between. Time telescoped; senses fused; the girlies on the screen, arms laced around bare waists, kicked their legs in unison and the music to which they danced beat and blazed away inside one's head, unheard by any but oneself, privately wired to each set of auditory nerves.

In my lap lay Tom Wolfe's new book about Ken Kesey, King of the Hippies — that book I'd rather have been reading than watching the film — in which I had read, perhaps a thousand miles ago, Ken Kesey saying ". . . forms of expression in which there will be no separation between myself and the audience. It will be all one experience, with all the senses opened wide, words, music, lights, sound, touch — lightning."

ALL ONE EXPERIENCE: NO SEPARATION. It might not be exactly what Ken Kesey had had in mind, but something very like it was going on right here inside our plane; precious little separated time or continents or music-making, the start of our adventure or whatever it was toward which we were flying.

Time folded up flat. Dissolved. All light had drained from the bowl of space outside the windows; it was night. A changed sense of one's own weight, a different level of sound in the ears, and we were making our descent into Brussels. Jack Kirkman of Philharmonic Hall, who functioned as special assistant to Bernstein on the tour — a young man with curly red hair and brown eyes who looked as if he should be dancing *L'Après-midi d'un Faune,* yet was to be one of the staunch mainstays of the tour — came up and handed Maestro his personal dressing case and packed the Mahler score away. Jamie folded up the sheets and sheets of whatever she had been writing and the pilots made a dream-landing — a perfect *atterrissage,* as French says it with such exquisite rightness, a "to-earthment" — at which all the musicians broke into spontaneous applause. Would they do this at every landing? Was this very American exuberance, this starting-out-on-holiday mood, now flaring up on arrival, to last?

A crowd of a hundred or more streamed toward the plane, and we walked down in a blinding blaze of light to the whirring cameras, outstretched hands, upturned faces of greeting; and Bernstein, an arm around each of his children, was swept away to the press interview.

Glimmering new NATO and World Bank buildings, shadowy rows of prosperous old burghers' houses flashed by in the night, and we were in an Old World hotel: wardrobes instead of closets and heavy silk curtains drawn across the windows, on the floor beside each bed a fresh towel to step out onto (who presses them?) On top of the bed — oh no — a lumpy mountain range of a featherbed. (Isn't it too hot? What season is this? What time of day? Where?) Down in the lobby, almost empty except for some of our companions and one or two sleepy-looking waiters, cocoa and sandwiches (the stomach says it is hours since food) with Willie Weissel and Paige Brook, flautist; Harold Gomberg, our great oboist, stopping by with a greeting, others passing and repassing. Brook (now there's exactly the right name for a flute player) in a mood of mellow, somewhat ribald reminiscence, his stories beginning clearly and cleverly but running out into ornate cadenzas, little spreading rivulets that disappear. Could it be me, and my wavering attention? And why is everything in these surroundings so vague and dim and underwater heavy, while we are all wide awake and witty . . .

Like all jet travelers we had invaded a different "here," still clothed in the matrix of "there" — as a diver entering water comes sheathed in a skin of air bubbles. We were a multiple intrusion of new presences, displacing an existing element. What's more, "we" (whatever it is that counts most) were not here yet at all but somewhere far behind, among those sunset clouds over the blue herringbone sea, listening to Mahler's Fourth and the Hard Rock in the earphones, even though Brussels trolley cars and buses were to batter our sleep throughout what remained of the night.

II

Belgium

THE FIRST DAY ABROAD of the tour was marked on the schedule Free Day. There were — I had counted them like so many unset jewels — just five of these, although for Amyas and me and much more so for Bernstein, they were seldom wholly free, with some official function at midday or cocktail time to split them apart. Today, after an early morning briefing from Nick and Willie, we measured out kilometers and hours available to us before a six o'clock reception and left for Bruges.

It was many years since I had been in Belgium and my memories of that visit were mostly of wet cobblestones, rain, and a rather gray human atmosphere as well, in which dinner with a spritely old couple (now dead) shone with as many golden glints as the gilt in the Grand' Place. Bruges had been the objective then, too, as I set out from Brussels with our two teen-age daughters, in the small car we had driven all the way from Genoa, on a tiresome rainy drive along a two-lane highway through one drab village after another. We had got no farther than Ghent, where the younger daughter collapsed from exhaustion, and we had driven back to Brussels, passing on the way a car like our own skidded off the road and overturned against a wall. I still longed to see Bruges.

It didn't seem the same country at all, this twenty-third day of August, fourteen years and a World's Fair later. A six-lane divided highway swept out of an enormous modern city, and after little more than an hour of whizzing past all those villages, through a countryside rich with crops and cattle and flowers, we were there. It was a kindly sunny day — the only one in weeks, it seemed — and Bruges, from the first sight of its spires at the bottom of a vast tender sky in which one sensed the nearness of the sea, was all summer gentleness and intimacy.

Since early the day before we had been flying, driving, hurrying, awake and asleep. Now we slowed down, even in the car, to a walker's pace in order to squeeze into the old town, contained and defined by its small spaces and narrow streets, its brick-lined canals brushed by the green hair of drooping trees. We stopped at last beside a small park where ducks stood preening on the grass, and our driver led us into a diminutive shop. Here two elderly women sat making *point de fée* lace. Not a sound except the clicking and clacking of bobbins — as fast as any woodpecker's hammering, more intricate than any fugue. We drew close to watch the cobweb design of deer and rabbits and birds growing from under the women's fingers as slowly as flowers (at most, an inch a day, someone said). Beautiful skill, which developed out of a "pass-time" (!), now dying out faster and faster and taught in schools to a diminishing number of pupils. Several other people stood watching like us in a trance, and when they first stirred and looked up, we all laughed: there were

William Nowinski, first violin, Ralph Mendelson, viola, his wife Joyce, another first violin, and Phyllis Wright, harpist. Finding each other in the same ten-by-twenty-foot shop made it seem as though other bobbins were flickering around somewhere, at work on unforeknown designs. As we crossed the canal together on our way to the famous "Béguinage," a sightseeing boat puttered under the bridge beneath us and one of the passengers called out. "Willie! It's Willie!" they exclaimed, leaning over the bridge wall and waving to Dembinsky, another violinist, as he reappeared below them, the water-light flickering on his travel-weary face.

The Béguinage, that peaceful enclave ringed around with little homes for elderly women, felt no more real than a postcard when we entered it. It was there, we were somewhere else. Impossible at first to stand still, or listen, or look — let alone see. Then wind from somewhere entered the upper reaches of the seventy-five-foot poplars standing in formal rows, and the sound of it was beautiful, steady and gentle, weirdly multiple for the myriads of separately twirling leaves. Though it went on playing high overhead, where we stood below, inside the embracing walls, we felt no wind at all. From the open door of the church came the voices of a choir of nuns. We stood and listened, passed on, walked along the cobbled path skirting the houses — each with its own charming detail of a statue in a niche, an unusual carved door or glimpse into a garden — while at our sides grass tall and soft as in a meadow spread away under the great trees, which in slow and stately dance kept changing their positions and the vistas seen between them.

Beside a dovecote, where white fantail pigeons murmured and fluttered, we looked back. The nuns were walking away from the church in their blue dresses and long white coifs, narrow and pointed as the wings of a tern, sunlight edging each coif with white radiance. Gracious, silent, anonymous figures, as at one with their surroundings as the trees and grass. Slowly the just-rightness of the pensionnaires' houses impressed itself, the mysterious beauty of enclosed space filled one like breath. Like all great forms — sonnet or sonata — grace is given by limitation itself; yet inside these walls are wind and sky, grass and shade, space and proportion. Here one could be content, with no need to go farther than the bridge across the canal, its swans now spread like powder puffs on the noon grass and the city only a murmur beyond the walls, trickled through from time to time with bells.

Such peace isn't quite real. Something has to smash its surface, and something did. We had been warned that the anti-French feeling in Flanders was very bitter and never to speak French there, but I had forgotten. Getting no response to a question I asked in English of a woman who seemed to belong there, I repeated it in French. At once her face tightened to a mask. I tried German. Wasn't it closer to Flemish, mightn't she get the drift? If she did, no hint of understanding was allowed to show in a face deliberately and tightly slammed shut. Not only was whatever might have passed between us so dead that even sign language and a smile failed to revive it, but some potentially violent presence had intruded itself, like a very small, very poisonous viper. A trifling incident, no more than the sound of glass breaking, but the first note of a theme we were to hear over and over in one country after another, growing sometimes in ominous crescendos: the theme of hate.

I began looking at nontourists with curiosity. What were they feeling, the man in the flower shop where we asked the way, the cathedral custodian, the people lunching in the canalside restaurant? Sitting in window alcoves, faces lit from the water below, they looked straight out of Flemish paintings — the young women with fair skin and high breasts and hair piled high and men with fleshy lips and florid coloring, but it was the older women with their square bodies and austere expressions who gave one thought, and as the day progressed we saw more and more of them. They must be the housewives responsible for all those scrubbed tiles everywhere and for the gleaming little panes of glass which light the housefronts on street or canal as if with sequins. Are they responsible, too, for keeping sharp the old and bitter feud splitting Belgium in two? This centuries-old animosity between Walloon and Fleming, between the more Celtic Belgians living nearer to France and those of Germanic descent in the northern and western part of the country, not only continues but is apparently worsening. On the night of our concert in Brussels, presented as part of the Festival of Flanders, we were to be told by more than one public personage that days of fence-mending would inevitably follow their appearing at a Flemish event.

After a stroll in the ancient city there was just time to see the great Memlings in the old hospital, that roomful of visual poems where Memling painted even the larger figures under a magnifying lens, putting in details with a brush made of a single hair, giving roundness and sheen to a soldier's armor by painting onto its surfaces the tiny, curving reflections of adjacent figures. What intensity of vision, what a sense of here-and-now — of a different order altogether than yesterday's, on the flight. The opposite pole from the contemporary grasping inclusion of space and sense impressions, avid as the mouths of jet engines gulping air.

Our own grasping sent us back along the freeway at seventy miles an hour to attend the reception in honor of Bernstein. He came and stood in the receiving line but would have been better to stay in bed since he had been felled by some virus overnight and was running a temperature. We had a doctor in our party, Paul Zea, very skillful at treating Bernstein's sometimes troublesome back. A huge and handsome man with white hair and thick black brows over dark eyes, he was keeping an uneasy watch over his charge, looking like an anxious brigand standing guard over treasure. The Salle Gallois filled with a steadily growing crowd through which harassed waiters struggled to find a way, holding aloft vast trays of delectables that were barely sampled. Bernstein, between his host, the American chargé d'affaires and the latter's handsome French wife, seemed to be his usual magnetic self in spite of the increasing babel and heat and his own fever but, like someone in a gangster movie, he was converged on from two directions at once by Amyas and by Zea, who, with apologies to their country's government, helped him to leave.

Next morning there was a rehearsal, one of only three scheduled for the tour. Because of the ten countries and eighteen cities we were to visit, the repertoire was kept to two and a half programs, which, by recombining, really made three different concerts. There were two very long, very demanding symphonies (Mahler's Fifth and Berlioz's *Fantastique*), two short symphonies by living composers (Roy Harris's Third and William Schuman's Third), and two openers (Haydn's Symphony No. 87 and Rossini's Overture to *L'Italiana in Algeri*). These had all been rehearsed in New York before leaving, but now there was a run-through to offset the flight and warm everyone up.

We didn't attend. Instead, and with what seemed like half of the population of Brussels, we went out to the Bois de la Cambre on a second cloudless day with a fresh undercurrent of air from the sea. Everywhere among the monumental trees and on the wide green perspectives between, people strolled or lay in deck chairs, rode bicycles or horses, played games. All the ages and stages of Man were there, from the peach-skinned babies being wheeled about with striped parasols clipped to their prams, to the monolithic, severe-faced grandmothers accompanying young families or sitting alone on folding chairs, furiously knitting, to the very old, failing parents, cared for by the middle-aged; while all through, live as exposed wires, ran roving bands of hoarse, rough boys, and lovers lay turned to their own world. There, spread out, was the whole frieze of our earthly existence, a living illustration of how alike we all are in our bodies and their destiny. *Why*, it made one want to cry out, why, when we know this in our blood, do we go on being so fiendish to each other?

The first concert, Haydn and Mahler, took place that night in Ghent. Arriving early at the little old Royal Opera House (it seats 1300), we had time to talk to some of the musicians who were waiting around outside the enclosed truck entrance which served them that night as a communal dressing room. They had an air of excitement mixed with apprehension — the hall was very small, had we been inside yet? They didn't know about the Mahler in there, the stage had been hard to set up, and Lenny, Lenny was feeling poorly.

They needn't have worried. That first concert was an epiphany — no other word for it — and Bernstein, though still feverish and taking antibiotics, rose and rose from one glory of music to another and took us all with him. The orchestra, moved by his love of Mahler and by their love for him, especially poignant on this the eve of his fiftieth birthday, dedicated themselves to playing better than their ordinary, very fine best. There is a mystery here, for later performances may have been even finer and even more musically perfect, yet this one established itself at once in some special place of its own, so that for the rest of the tour, when any comparing and analyzing of performances was going on, people would say: of course, at *Ghent*, now . . .

This made itself clear from the first notes of the Haydn — so elate and graceful, so full of verve, and particularly right in that intimately enclosing Opera House in which a single gently plucked violin gives off warmest reverberations. Haydn might have composed the Eighty-seventh precisely for this hall, just as the oboe solo in the third movement's Trio seemed created for Harold Gomberg. A great and impassioned artist, Harold appears to live in some other world than ours, obsessed with fashioning always better and cleaner reeds and further refining his tone, wrestling day and night with perfection's angel, and its demons. He is wonderful to watch. Rubens would have liked to paint that handsome dark-haired opulence, the face rich in flesh and coloring, which — when in a demanding passage it swells and reddens and grows more chins and dimples than it already has — becomes the face of Aeolus blowing across old maps of the world. Only instead of raying outward, all that breath and intensity converges and focuses to produce a tone sharply tender, sweet but with a bite in it and always so controlled a single note or phrase will grow and grow, be held, die away to nothing — all on one taken breath. It was fitting, when Bernstein had taken his calls and motioned Gomberg to rise, that the applause clattered to a new high.

But we were nervous after the Haydn and its small orchestra. Wouldn't the Mahler be just too much in here? The *fortissimi* overwhelming? It wasn't, they weren't. Comfortably alcoved in our red damask boxes (seating only four apiece) we were carried on streams and clouds of sound, we were contained at the heart of the music, we heard the slightest nuance of a single instrument and all the lights and shadings of the ensembles. (Nowhere on the tour, by the way, did the acoustics seem finer than in the old opera houses with their horseshoes of boxes, and in only two halls as fine. I say "seem" advisedly, because we were to discover wide variations of opinion on this slippery subject.) It is notable, too, how well one hears concerts from a box — at least I do. Though I don't like to admit this, my listening is much affected by those around me. If they are attentive, better yet, creative listeners, my own hearing is enhanced, like playing tennis with someone better than oneself; but if they are at all restless, their energy dissipated in any of what Amyas calls the seven deadly concert sins, my own listening suffers. The Ghent audience was a breath-held one, one could have sat anywhere, but our box was an added pleasure for sharing it with the wife of our cultural attaché in Brussels and, as we learned, a lieder singer who sings many Mahler songs.

Mahler's Fifth had new associations for Bernstein and for the string section of the orchestra. On that terrible and recent June seventh he had received a call in his New York studio from Air Force One, the plane bringing Robert Kennedy's body home: a member of the family begged that he and the New York Philharmonic play at the Funeral Mass. What they played was the Adagietto from the Fifth Symphony. No one who watched this, I think, will forget that musical interlude, played while ten Kennedy children, including those of the dead President, carried the sacraments to the high altar. It is music of purest peace and sorrowing gentleness, eleven and a half minutes of repeated reflection and lamentation on the part of sixty-eight stringed instruments — a kind of angels' lullaby brushing over you, sighing and mourning for your grief. It was sad to see (wherever it was played) that it put some people actually to sleep, and it must gradually have lost some of its poignancy for the orchestra, but that night in Ghent there were tears in the musicians' eyes and on their faces. Their memories of accompanying all those orphaned children were still strung with pain.

At the finish of the tremendous, hour-and-fourteen-minute symphony there was a long moment of stunned silence, then the audience exploded into applause. "And they are usually very undemonstrative here!" we were told again and again in delighted surprise. How Bernstein, still ill, survived his normally strenuous conducting none of us knew, least of all Dr. Zea, who shook his head and made dark looks as he watched that nearly beaten-looking man walk offstage in a daze, wet hair clinging to his head. A few minutes later, the musicians were climbing into buses for the drive back to Brussels, excited and happy, a little astonished (we felt) that it had gone *that* well. I felt sorry for them with such a long drive ahead, but then, our day was not over either, nor was it for the Maestro, who in spite of his doctor went to the party in his honor.

We were to go to at least one party a day, few of which will be mentioned in these pages since large formal receptions are so much alike; but this, according to a card sent to us by our official hosts, the Festival of Flanders, was "an intimate dinner party for which Baron F. Verhaegen, Oude Houtlei

No. 60, is making his magnificent residence available." The adjective, well meant, was wrong. That eighteenth-century town house was better than "magnificent," just as its owner, the Baron, and his family are aristocrats in a sense not always conveyed by that word. "A beautiful man," as Bernstein said later of our host, and his Swedish-born wife and the two of their six grown children whom we met were beautiful too — inside and out.

The house was both formal and cozy, full of books and portraits and oriental rugs like flowered lawns underfoot, with a salon of brocade-covered walls where a fire burned gently on a Renaissance hearth and a rough-haired dachshund named "Taxi" took overmuch charge of arriving guests. We had walked out into the garden, with its small fountain and orangerie, and were sitting around the fire talking when there came the unmistakable galvanization and suddenly electric atmosphere of Bernstein's entering the house and then the room. He was wearing the wide black evening cape left to him by Koussevitsky; someone took this for him and he moved around the room greeting and meeting. It is fascinating to feel the change of spirit in any room he comes into, particularly right after a concert. Something more than admiration and awe of his celebrity takes over: there is a definite sense of exhilaration — partly because of having had one's emotions so invited, and released, by the concert itself, partly because it raises the temperature of feeling to be near anyone so intensely alive and expressive. That night, there was also concern. "He gives *so much* of himself," the Baron said to me, "how will he stand five weeks of it?" Perhaps, too, since conductors like actors seem to be larger than life, even sorcerers, people are surprised, after such an experience as we had just been given, to meet a man of medium height with eyes that are tired, often sad. This giant, this magician, who just now from the podium called for — and *got* — all that thunder and lightning and aching sweetness, wants a scotch-and-water, a place to sit down, something to eat!

It is rare to eat as we did that evening — cold trout under a delicate sauce, thin slices of breast of chicken surrounded with sweetbreads and mushrooms, and pastry cornucopias spilling out marble-sized potatoes and peas, a mocha mousse inside a baroque montage of ice cream and vanilla fingers with a lyre, in chocolate, on the summit. There were three tables for eight in a room lit entirely by candles; we were served by elderly family servants.

The Baron, from whose feet Taxi went out to investigate all the feet collected around him, made a touching speech in English for which he need not have made the apology he did. An educated foreigner's slightly unusual turn of phrase or unexpected choice of a word gives whatever is being said an endearing genuineness like that of handmade articles; it makes one's own language sound suddenly surprising and new. Bernstein replied with gentle deliberateness, picking his words carefully and lovingly, giving them, as he always does, an almost musical stress. He finished on a sad note. Acknowledging that the orchestra was his country's ambassador, he spoke of "our great country — or rather our country which *could* be so great — and for the time being isn't." Soon afterwards, Amyas gave gracious thanks but said he must care for our chief asset and take him home. I'm not sure the "chief asset" liked it, even though ill; when he is well, being with people he enjoys restores and revives him, giving whatever power drives him fresh outlets for its forces.

As it turned out, he had an outlet even so, for on the sixty-mile drive back to Brussels he gave us quite a brilliant sketch of Israel and of what Amyas and I should do and see in the two days we were to be there on our own. Above all else we must try to spend a night in a kibbutz, he urged us; it would be an experience we would never forget. "There's such spirit in them, among the young people particularly. They sing from morning till night. That's *one* country where everyone is full of hope and optimism, and it's contagious. There is music all the time. Try to stay at Ein Gev — that's the kibbutz at the foot of the Golan Heights." And he described how life had gone on there throughout years of intermittent bombardment from the Syrian batteries overhead, though when they finally saw what was up there, after the six-day war, they admitted they would never have dared to stay.

He laid out a detailed tour for us: Haifa, "another Naples, but in that wonderful light," Nazareth, now a Christian Arab city, and on to Kinneret (in Galilee), Capernaum, and "oh be sure to swim in the Sea of Galilee! Later, when you go to the Dead Sea, swim in that too — if you can get yourself deep enough in the water — you'll come out all crusted thick with salt and they'll turn a hose on you." Jericho? Qumran? I asked. Hesitation. There were two kinds of sightseeing: historical-archaeological and experiential; it depended on which kind one preferred. A distinction I was to remember many times, not only in Israel but wherever we went, seeing fewer "sights," the more we experienced.

Back in the hotel lobby, empty except for a couple of night clerks behind the desk, he was afraid we might forget what he had told us, picked up a piece of paper from the counter and, noticing something written in one corner, held it up to the sleepy clerk. Important? No? Quickly he wrote down the key names, the manager of Ein Gev, the different towns.

We stepped into the elevator to get to our rooms. It was already August twenty-fifth, his fiftieth birthday; it had been for two and a half hours, but all three of us acted as if it were still yesterday.

III

Happy Birthday

THERE WAS A SPECIAL, very large trunk in the Philharmonic's twenty thousand pounds of baggage: the Loot Trunk, in which were packed all the gifts presented along the way. Jack Kirkman was in charge of this, as he was of the Maestro's eight suitcases, his four "carry-on bags," and his entire wardrobe. Getting on and off planes, Jack moved inside his carefully distributed load like a willing packhorse along a precipice, but once checked in at a hotel he metamorphosed into a commanding general, an inspired diplomat. Every twenty-four hours there were two more full-dress shirts and a tuxedo shirt as well as sport shirts to be laundered; jackets, trousers, tail suits to be pressed or cleaned (he had time for only a little pressing himself), and since he spoke no foreign language, these staggering requests often had to be acted out like charades. It seems he was never defeated, partly because he was studying to be an actor and threw himself into it, even more, I suspect, because of a personality and manner that could disarm even those high priests of unwillingness — hotel valets. After that one day of August twenty-fifth, the Loot Trunk was already over half full.

It was a curious day; perhaps all world celebrities' birthdays are. One has the impression that on top of the genuine warmth of personal feeling there is a collective, almost hysterical air of celebration as if everyone used the occasion to project his own ego, maybe even to congratulate himself on having made it this far. In Brussels that August twenty-fifth, emotions, nationalities, languages, gifts accumulated into a mad, overwrought babel. On the official level, there were ambassadors who were planning to be there but whom the Czech crisis obliged to be absent while our own ambassador, who had not expected to be present, returned. There were the Festival of Flanders people who were sponsoring the concert and Brussels people with anti-Flemish feelings. Radio and television pages of newspapers carried notices of simultaneous birthday programs in several countries. There was a birthday concert that night with a mammoth birthday party afterwards and, at noon, an informal gathering in Bernstein's suite when he got up which was like a royal levee. There we met the head of the Volksoper who had come from Vienna for the day, and musical personages from London, Berlin, Amsterdam, Italy. Gifts, cablegrams, flowers, letters covered every table and shelf, but the best present had arrived the day before when Bernstein gave reluctant permission to an unrecognized voice on the house telephone to bring up the gift she said she had for him and in walked the present herself, his old friend Vera Zorina, just arrived from New York.

The birthday concert — Rossini's Overture, Harris's Third, and Berlioz — was the antithesis of the previous night: sharp, brilliant, sensational. Bernstein's *Fantastique* is a gigantic tour de force, musically and dramatically, and the symphony itself a masterpiece of orchestral color and fire. The hall stayed brightly lit throughout the concert and the acoustics seemed to us over-brilliant — certainly not warm and enveloping as in Ghent.

I wondered how this audience would take to the Harris, a composition as American as our prairies and small Western towns, and was not surprised at the somewhat reserved applause. Maybe the increasing strain and anguish in the last part of the symphony, the progressively warped theme and the groaning horns culminating in three huge final bangs, is too deeply unsettling. It is a horrifying ending, without redemption. I could never hear those shocking booms except as reminders of our three assassinations. In the intermission, the Verhaegens — whom the Ghent concert had moved into coming tonight, too, though they had not planned to do so — told us they found it profoundly tragic music. Just then our ambassador approached, led Amyas and me away, and, introducing us to the Soviet ambassador, left us alone with him. A mild and pleasant-enough-looking man, yet how to behave with him? Indicate one's revulsion at what his country's government had just perpetrated, or assume he might be just as unhappy over that as we were about Vietnam? There could have been few living beings I wanted to meet less at that moment in time; a drop of gall in the day.

The birthday party, for more than four hundred, took time to assemble in a labyrinth of lobbies and corridors outside the ballroom of the Hilton. Somewhere in the wait I stood talking with two of our musicians — Myor Rosen, harpist, and Bob Johnson, a French horn player. Bob had a lot to say about the greatness of the orchestra; he believed it lies in its extraordinarily wide range of tone. "There is a dark sound and a bright sound," he explained, "and it is hard to move from one to another — particularly hard to move from bright to dark, so that one starts dark and moves toward brightness. Most orchestras settle into one sound," ran his theory, "either what you might call all silk or all velvet, but the Philharmonic makes both equally well and goes from one to the other as freely as the conductor wishes."

The door to the ballroom opened. The hundreds trickled in, dispersed, regathered at tables in a room chilled through but soon to be overhot. Two tables were reserved for dignitaries and for the guest of honor, who sat, we saw happily, between his two children, though in a blue-white blaze of TV illumination (we were to be "on," "live") and in an insectlike swarm of creeping, clambering photographers and glass-eyed cameras. There were, I think, ten speeches (magnificently short) each followed by the presentation of a gift, the order of these most carefully arranged according to protocol: State Department and Trans World Airlines, Festival of Flanders, Columbia Records, and so on. There was a ten-foot-high birthday cake, wheeled in by airline hostesses. There were sculptures of musicians in butter — remarkable creations which, as Lenny said later in his saddest voice, would have saved whole villages in Biafra from starving. Over all, the buzz of conversation echoed back from a lowish ceiling so that one could barely hear one's neighbor, and even with microphones and a lot of *sh-sh-sh*-ing only those close to the head tables really heard the speeches.

One thing, though, was heard by all. Last of the presentations came the gift from the members of the orchestra, presented by the head of the orchestra's committee, Selig Posner, viola. It was the facsimile score of Mahler's Tenth Symphony and once it was in Bernstein's hands, all over the room — wherever they were sitting — the musicians rose and, led by Posner, sang "Happy Birthday." Bernstein's eyes opened wide, his eyebrows peaked, he put the back of his hand to his mouth in utter unbelieving merriment: the one hundred and six voices were wildly out of tune. "Singing in twenty-eight keys!" he said later. He looked happier than he had all day.

Just before this Amyas, representing the Philharmonic Society, presented its gift. It was the smallest one given, in size and maybe in expense, though only the future can measure the size of its meaning. This was the last year of Bernstein's tenure as Music Director, his last tour with the orchestra in that capacity, but so close had the bond become that a new title of Laureate Conductor had been created for the new role he would have. As everyone interested knew, this multiple-talented genius wanted more leeway for composing; as not everyone appreciated, conducting — and especially conducting this particular orchestra — was also deeply important to him. He needed a podium from which to express music as well as time in which to create it, and this highly versatile instrument (with "both a silk and velvet sound") was just right for this need. Somehow this had to be expressed in the gift and in its presentation.

I watched Amyas get up and walk toward the microphone, one shoulder a bit hiked up as it often is at times of stress, and wondered how his gift would be received. It seemed so small, so uninspired, and who knew what was collecting in that trunk back at the hotel — besides the gifts here? The magnified voice, seeming to come from everywhere except the speaker, himself, said, "I have here a gift for Lenny from the New York Philharmonic Society — a small gift, a set of cufflinks to hold his sleeves together." The recipient raised his head, looked quizzical and amused. There was important symbolism in these links, these chains (the speaker continued); he had been shocked on arrival in Brussels to hear reporters assume that Bernstein was leaving the orchestra. This wasn't true; he was not leaving. As some wise man had said, it was good for a man, as for a plant, to be repotted from time to time, and this is what Lenny was doing as he entered his fifties: giving his roots more room. We had a new title for the new relationship with us. For his lifetime he was to be our Laureate Conductor — free to pursue his art, his interests. Since he would continue to do some conducting for us we had engraved on each link the symbol of the Society. "These links, by their smallness," he concluded, "symbolize his reduced obligation. Our true tie is one of love — a powerful tie because the New York Philharmonic is a close family."

How close a family was to be a continually unfolding revelation; without it, there would probably be no story of our symphonic journey. As for the cufflinks, often as the days and miles added up Lenny was to speak of how much he cared for them, though I don't believe any of us knew until John Gruen's book, *The Private World of Leonard Bernstein,* came out the following fall that another pair of cufflinks, Koussevitzky's, have always formed part of his preconducting ritual: he gives them a quick kiss before going onstage.

Leaving the party, we passed a group having a conspicuously good time together in a dim corner near the door: our concertmaster, David Nadien, and first cellist Lorne Munroe, violist Lincer with four other string players, and, in their midst, the Verhaegens. The Baron jumped up and thanked us warmly for these new good friends, then wished us success on the rest of the tour and in Israel. "At Cesarée," he added, to me. On my mentioning the night before at supper that we were to play in the Roman amphitheater at Caesarea, he had asked me if I knew Racine's lovely lines from "Bérénice":

> Dans l'Orient desert quel devint mon ennui!
> Je demeurais longtemps errant dans Cesarée,
> Lieux charmants ou mon coeur vous avait adorée.

Cesarée, Jerusalem, the kibbutz called Ein Gev. Next morning, Monday, the orchestra was leaving for Switzerland and a single concert in Lucerne; we were flying to Tel Aviv, where they would rejoin us on Wednesday. Back in our room where the bags were almost packed for early departure, cool clothes hanging in the wardrobe, for it was still dreadfully hot in Israel, I thought of Bruges and Ghent, Memling and Mahler, the woman with hate in her eyes — and Baron Verhaegen, moved by the music of Racine and of Roy Harris. We had now heard all except one piece of the repertoire but were still in the first country of ten to be visited, only four days out from home. How would it be possible, any more than it was for the Loot Trunk, to take in so much?

IV

Israel

GETTING FROM the northwest corner of Europe to the southeast corner of the Mediterranean took most of a day — one of those confused, limbolike days of jet travel, not quite long or unbroken enough for any real occupation as slower travel once was but an alternation of hurrying on foot down long monotonous tunnels of glass and sitting strapped to one place, in one position, hearing nothing for the sound of jets, and, in each airport, the interchangeable expressionless voice of flight announcers who, whether speaking in French, German, Italian, English, or Hebrew all talk the same nonlanguage with the same anticadences. On the Sabena plane we encountered more of the curious failure of communication we had found in Belgium. It was as hard to "get through" to stewardesses in the air as it had been to people on the ground. Perhaps it is that widening split between French and Flemish and the banked distrust which make for an almost schizoid withdrawnness and preoccupation.

To step out from this in its purest, canned concentration

and walk through tropic evening air into the crowded noisy Tel Aviv airport and be welcomed with cheerful *shaloms* was like going from a wintry house into a summer garden. Then, after one of those anxious night drives from a strange airport into a strange city (how far is it? isn't he driving awfully fast? is it really the best route?), after lobbies and elevators and corridors and more *shaloms*, we opened the door of our room to the balcony beyond it and were overwhelmed by the sustained roar, the warm dark breath of the Mediterranean far below. The stone railing was still warm under our hands from the day; long white scallops of surf unrolled for miles down the coast. I wanted to weep. This was the westernmost sea-rim of Asia, the new-old promised land, which, together with our other parent, Greece, is the source of our thought and spirit. That knowledge must lie deep in the mind's collective blood and bone to sweep me, half New Englander, half Dane as I am, with such a sense of recognition and belonging.

At midday next day we were on our way to Galilee, in an air-conditioned car driven by Joseph Nevo — thirty-five, stocky, and like all able-bodied Israelis a reserve in the armed forces. Official Israeli guides are very carefully picked and educated, and Joseph seemed to us a fine representative of his country, of that "steady virtue and dignity of mind" one feels in the Israelis. If he was without special style or graciousness, he also had none of the tired airs and guile of so many guides elsewhere but was forthright and eager and natural.

The first of many times he referred to the six-day war, I asked him what he did then.

"I was a paratrooper."

"Did you make many jumps?"

"No. I didn't jump myself. I arranged drops — of equipment, men, so on." He chuckled. "One of my assignments was a funny one. I had to drop two thousand breakfast rolls of a certain kind one morning in the Sinai Desert. They weren't out of bread down there but the commanding colonel had promised them to his men if they carried out a mission successfully, and they did. What a job! getting all those rolls baked and packaged for dropping — all in one night. But they got their rolls all right."

Joseph talked a great deal about the war and its aftermath; such things as Israel's now allowing Syrian and Jordanian Arabs to visit their relatives at will though Israelis could never go *there,* or the Jordanians always shooting first along the cease-fire line, the Israelis only returning the fire. He exuded conviction and confidence while never denying the extremity of the situation which through the days grew almost visible, as if a mountain massif high as the Andes reared up in that blue air. Patriotism animated everything he said, yet without doubting him I couldn't quite believe anything was as simple as he suggested, nor that all the virtue was on one side. For that matter, in spite of his patriotic enthusiasm Joseph showed a certain warmth toward the Arabs, even a wistful envy of their way of life. When we passed a Bedouin encampment at dusk, he broke out, "Look at them there, sitting out drinking their tea and enjoying the evening. They have no ambition but no heart attacks or ulcers either. Makes you wonder about our way of life, doesn't it? Maybe theirs is better after all."

Joseph had the virtue, most unusual in a guide, of being sensitive to his clients' individual interests and idiosyncrasies. Very well informed and explicit about historical and archaeological facts, he also picked up quickly and acted on our fondness for "experiential sightseeing," stopping to examine unusual flowers, once to pick a strange pod off a tree beside the road. He brushed the dust off it and handed it to us to eat. Did we know what it was? No? St. John's Bread — what Saint John the Baptist ate in the wilderness. We found its chewy texture and sweetish datelike flavor delicious. We also stopped for a lot of picture-taking, Joseph being as enthusiastic about photography as Amyas.

Even without such stops, however, there wasn't enough time to go as far north as Haifa; the countryside was much too beautiful to speed through. Everywhere, rolling away to the horizon or the shore, magnificent farming: the richest-looking earth, striped with gleaming aluminum irrigation pipes and fans of sprinkled water; near the sea, cypresses or cane windbreaks protecting orange groves, peach and pomegranate orchards, banana plantations; farther inland, fields of artichokes, tomatoes, corn, wheat, vineyards, cows and sheep and goats; and all this in what twenty years ago was desert. Partway down the long descent from Nazareth to Galilee — six hundred feet below sea level — where that peacock-blue water first appears, the road passes between a hill on one side so thick with boulders and ledges there is barely any visible earth and, on the other, a sweeping valley now tilled and watered but so recently desert that there were (then) lines of boulders waiting to be trucked away. Joseph said they would be gone within a month and, from what we kept observing of Israeli enterprise, no doubt they were.

Nor did we get to spend the night at Ein Gev (you didn't do *anything* I told you to, Lenny accused us), staying instead at Tiberias directly across from it. But we did swim in the Sea. The evening of our arrival (like every summer evening, Joseph said) there "came down a storm of wind on the lake," a "boisterous wind," rushing in from the colder heights of Lebanon to fill the space left by the day's rising heat, brushing the water a violently deep blue. With darkness the wind died and in the early morning, when we bathed, the water was warm and still; a haze veiled the Golan Heights on the far shore, and in the hotel garden sprinklers clicked and shushed and small birds fluttered in the whisking drops. It was almost as tranquil as it must have been on mornings nineteen hundred and forty years before, when Christ walked along the shore and called out to Simon and Andrew as they cast their nets . . .

The quiet was ripped open by two jet fighters whistling from over the mountain and into a roaring sweep toward the Jordan valley, then turning, lifting — noiseless, now — over the Golan Heights to dissolve from sight high over Capernaum. Capernaum, where the multitudes came and were fed; where now congregations of little gold birds sway and sing in the windy trees, and some of the great stone fragments from the Temple, when they are struck with another stone, ring like bells. For an hour or more, now, jets in pairs made their southward sweeps, banking steeply back and "taking a look around," as Joseph said, adding, "on Monday there was some shooting from Jordan."

The spirit of Ein Gev, as Lenny had said, was indeed extraordinary. The manager, Ben Joseph (brother of Yale's Professor Goldschmidt, then an economic adviser at the White House), walked around with us, showing us the simple, good living quarters, the music auditorium and restaurant, the babies' and small children's nurseries. Everyone we saw along the way was busy and cheerful — too engaged in the community work and too self-sufficient to notice tourists unless stopped and introduced. The grounds, reclaimed from desert, are by this time like a park, green and shady with large date palms and fruit trees, though trenches leading to a complete underground settlement are still there and ventilators thrust up like metal mushrooms in the shrubbery. Till June 1967 there was hardly a day the people of the kibbutz didn't have to make use of them. If more than a day had to be spent underground, someone would volunteer to creep out at night and water the fruit trees and gardens.

I asked Ben Joseph about the young people in the kibbutz — were there many rebels?

"Hippies?" He smiled. "No. They are freer here — like everywhere else — than they used to be, but they are not extreme. We try to listen to them; it is very important to hear and understand them because, you see," he stopped walking a moment, looking inward, "they are the generation of changing reality."

South of Ein Gev there is a half-mile-wide strip of cultivated land between the lake and the heights where farmers have built primitive shelters, like a mole's humps, to jump into from their tractors in case of attack. The heights end at the Yarmuk River valley where the road east crosses the old Syrian border, passing through a dreadful landscape — vast and barren and desolate, past mined fields and deserted villages, under cliffs and crags to which, if you look carefully, pillboxes cling like horrible concrete lichen. Only army vehicles were on the road that morning, and where the final one-way climb to the heights began we had to turn back. South again, now, beside the Jordanian border, past fields being farmed, tanks and half-tracks standing under trees, jeeps filled with soldiers on the road. Joseph pointed out a kibbutz between us and the river: seven casualties there last week; a factory out of commission, its roof a charred wreck; and the wall of a bridge we crossed, loose chunks of its concrete dangling from metal ribs. "That happened Monday," he said, and to reassure us, "I checked again this morning and we knocked out all their batteries; this is much the safest time — right after a shooting."

Just the same, it was good to reach Beit Shean and turn westward into the beautiful Ysreel valley — to see once again other than military vehicles and pass children and women on the roadsides, to get out of the car and stand in the fragrant wind blowing over that rich and fertile land. Best of all, at the afternoon's end, back in the glittering hive of our hotel, to greet the travelers coming in, like us forty-eight hours earlier, from the warm dark: Lenny, followed by Jamie with her neat, scrubbed look, the small round of her face touchingly pale, "Axel," wearing a jaunty Tyrolean hat, grave Anatole Heller, foreign agent of the whole tour, and Jack, burdened and rumpled and smiling. Behind them, in groups and singly, came all the rest, each stopping at a table to pick up his room key and mail in an envelope marked with his name. I was beginning to recognize a few more by now, but they were still a big crowd and I was surprised by how good it felt to be together again.

Of the two ways to see new places — "reading up" beforehand or going and looking and then reading afterwards — there is a lot to be said for the second, for however much he protests to the contrary, no adult travels without some associations, some residue of memories, not *of* but about places, which gather flavor in the dark of time like fruits in brandy. The depth of focus these memories give to the surface of reality seems somehow greater than that of newly acquired knowledge; there is both more surprise and more seasoned familiarity.

Everyone of my generation, I suppose, grew up with pictures of the Holy Land — sepia photographs on classroom walls, crudely colored ones in Bibles which, for art lovers, became transformed by the Biblical landscapes and scenes of great paintings. Those huddled cubes of houses around domes and minarets, shepherds resting under olive trees with their flocks, are all there in the mind's eye. What I wasn't prepared for, not having reviewed any history before going, was the accumulation of Jerusalem, so great that it makes Rome seem almost simple. In the Dome of the Rock, that glittering temple enshrining the rock on which Abraham stood with his knife over Isaac, there is a place where you may reach into the dark and feel the footprint left by Mohammed as he ascended into heaven. All Jerusalem, more than any city I know, bears footprints — of Jews, Mohammedans, Christians, Crusaders, of what feels like every nation and religious sect on earth. Walls are built and torn down or blown up or walled in, and re-exposed and rebuilt again; the city, as Jesus prophesied when he rode into it on the last Sabbath of his life, has had its enemies "cast a trench about it, surround it on every side." The book of Isaiah which was entombed in a Dead Sea cave and refound by a goatherd is enshrined in a monument not only to Biblical text but to twentieth-century architecture, while next to it the sculpture collection of an American Jew who made millions in entertainment is glorified in a hillside garden designed by a Japanese artist. It feels like the navel of the world here — the dim tunnels and arcades of the Old City a seethe of people and civilizations through which donkeys loaded with rubble from the latest war delicately tap their way. Seen from any distance, the city on its many hills shines in a glory of light like the Greek light, only greater, and seems to float in the sky. This radiance, and airiness, together with the press of accumulation are as unexpected to the newcomer as is the warm color of the city as a whole — not tawny dark like Rome but a clear pale gold. In spite of myself, "Jerusalem the Golden" kept singing inside my head; the city made me feel worshipful and hungry for knowledge.

The mayor, Teddy Kollek, received a few of us before the concert. "Teddy's?" Joseph repeated (it seems everyone calls him Teddy) yes, he knew where it was, and driving us to the end of a tree-lined street showed us into a small apartment house. The hall was dark as the night outside but a time-switch gave light long enough for us to climb the stairway to the fourth floor. A young man in blue jeans opened the door, and for the half hour or so we were there other equally casually dressed very young men answered telephones and came in and out of the room with messages. The Mayor, though in the midst of a personal crisis for which he apologized — his mother was very ill — showed the personal attentiveness and warmth for which he is so loved. A big, solidly built man in shirtsleeves, light brown hair disheveled, he moved around the room open and welcoming as an open fire, his large hands quick to rest on a shoulder or arm, attentive to each of us in turn. One could see why he gave the citizens of Jerusalem such comfort in the six-day war — taking immediate charge of broken water mains or heartbroken people, removing barbed wire and barricades as quickly as possible so as to open the divided city to itself.

The concert took place in the new, barely finished Binyanei Ha'ooma, a prominent hall on a high hill, reminiscent in architecture of Philharmonic Hall back in New York and with what seemed to Amyas and me some of the same faults in tone. Perhaps this will be modified; it was still so new then that the outdoor approaches weren't finished and the audience had to walk hundreds of yards across rough ground to get to it. A great many important people were there, including the President of Israel and Abba Eban, foreign minister, but it was an informal audience, enormously eager, talkative and with the vitality and heartiness of the frontier over it. Not far from us, in the same row with Jamie and Alexander, sat our driver, Joseph, discreetly taking photographs, very excited. Since a narrow extension of the balcony surrounds the whole stage, we looked right into the faces of people seated above the brass section and in turn facing Bernstein. One young couple kept looking at one another to share their feeling and were a study of entrancement; almost everyone sat forward at an extreme angle — immobile, deeply moved.

We were brought to our feet at the concert's start by the national anthem, ponderous, tragic, Biblical in its dignity and intensity. Pause. "The Star-Spangled Banner." I could scarcely believe what I heard. Was it really *that* bouncy and jingly and trivial? No happier than most people about its being our national anthem, tonight I was appalled by the contrast; it was a tune made up by kids on a picnic — not very talented ones, either.

The Haydn sounded foreign in another way, its delicate precision in curious counterpoint to a country of such contrasts and tensions But the Mahler — that was different. It is music that, even when it is being gay and gentle, feels dragged out of the depths, joy flowering in despair; one was sure these people would identify with it. They did, and the audience gave Bernstein, who had conducted here two months before and had celebrated the reunification with a concert on Mount Scopus, a tremendous response. Yet the performance was not what it had been at Ghent. Next evening he said to me, "I conducted badly last night." It seems he was concerned about the children; the nights were worse than usual.

Alexander, like his father, never got enough sleep, nor could he make up for it in the daytime; yet he came with Jamie to every concert and stayed to the end. They knew exactly how it was going, hearing such rare "bobbles" as occurred and being aware of any variations in their father's conducting. Long before the applause at intermission declined, they were picking their way carefully past their neighbors to get backstage to see him — Jamie usually dressed in long-sleeved white, Axel's clothes as neat as a pin but all of his still-small frame and beautiful, expressive face charged with excitement. Sometimes, while following the music, sitting way forward in his seat, he couldn't hold it all in and conducted a few phrases himself.

After that night's concert we were once more guests of the Mayor, at a supper for about twenty guests on the outdoor roof of a hotel in the Arab quarter. Although the hotel itself had seen better times the food was superlative and there was a comfortable flexibility to the party, through which the Mayor went table-hopping, never sitting down to eat but giving of himself to each person there. (To Bernstein, whom he enveloped in a huge hug on his arrival, he presented a 700 B.C. figurine of a lute player, found on Cyprus.) Meanwhile, at the simplest undecorated table and from very plain china we scooped onto pieces of Arab bread delicacies whose ingredients I couldn't guess, among them *humus*, that paste of ground chick-peas and sesame and peanut which is smooth as cream cheese and tastes like an essence of earth as clams do of the sea; these dishes — hors d'oeuvres only — followed by nuggets of grilled meat and chops of day-old lamb eaten in one's fingers. Could there be perhaps some inverse ratio law affecting the food of those restaurants that spend thousands on advertising their decor?

The next night we dined at an even simpler place on a dingy street in old Jaffa with Lenny, Azariah Rappaport, who had been his bodyguard and aide in the 1948 war, and his wife, and the pianist Ruth Menzies Cohen. It was one of those places which if you walked past it in the street you would hardly know to be a restaurant, and to get to its few tables out in a small courtyard you pass through the kitchen. The cooking and serving was all done by members of one Arab family. Even the old grandfather found small ways to help when he wasn't sitting smoking his hookah under a great tree whose branches stretched over all the diners. The branches were, as well, the refuge and playground of families of cats: cats asleep in crotches, kittens chasing one another up and down the highways of the slanting trunk or batting at the tree's long beanlike pods, two cats having a terrible fight. Even in this unlikely place Bernstein was recognized and had barely sat down when a woman came up and begged in a harsh Midwestern voice to take his picture. He nodded but asked her to wait till later. Having at last taken it, she handed the camera to her husband, came over and squatted beside Bernstein, getting her head as close to his as possible, and the shutter was snapped again.

"She had her nerve," I exploded, when she had bounced off. "You were very forgiving, it seems to me."

He dragged on his cigarette and looked off into the jungle of the tree. "What can you do? You have to realize what that picture *could* mean to her."

But later in the evening when a man approached saying,

"I *hate* to interrupt, but . . ." he growled back, "Why do it, then?" The first intruder had at least been sincere.

The last day in Israel began badly. I was still in bed, eating my breakfast yogurt and honey and cheese when "W," as Willie Weissel calls himself, rang up and said he must see us at once. One of the horn players, it seemed, was critically ill in the hospital. While we had been eating and drinking and laughing under the tree, he had been found in his room unconscious and in convulsions. On admission to the hospital he had been given three hours to live. This morning he was miraculously better, but W had spent most of the night setting in motion what had to be done. The man's wife was already on her way to Tel Aviv and Willie would go to the airport to meet her. One of the doctors in attendance was ready to fly back with the sick man to New York in a few days if it was thought best to return him there; this was what in fact happened, after arrangements that took care of every contingency and human consideration. When the rest of us left Israel, Ken Haas — all six feet seven of him, "in charge of things that come up" — stayed behind to see that whatever could be controlled was. But there was a sadness over the musicians, especially that group sitting between the trumpets at the back and the woodwinds in front.

That night the concert was at Caesarea, forty miles north of Tel Aviv, in the Roman theater that was excavated twelve years before and was still being restored. For all those centuries it had lain buried under a sand dune, until a farmer, plowing, struck the very top row of seats with his tractor.

We approached it by a road running right beside the sea and past the Crusaders' city. Under strong searchlights its walls and battlements and watchtowers stood out against the night sky; waves rushed the seawall and charged noisily up the beach in ranks of blazing white.

The night was very warm but at the top of the theater there was enough breeze to wave the banners there. Archways and lintels of huge stones, all the approaches shone in the illumination a warm deep honey color; the half moon, three quarters of the way down the western sky, was coldly blue over small drifts of cloud. In the theater itself men in shirtsleeves, women in summer dresses filled solidly the steep wall of stone steps; from our seats on the theater floor the sound of their voices made a loud rustle, like wind in a wood, through which single words could be clearly heard.

At earlier concerts here we had been told the wind had sometimes blown the music away from the "people wall" at the back and out to sea. This concert, put on as part of the Israel Festival celebrating Israel's twentieth year, was the first in which a newly constructed shell was used over the stage. Ingeniously engineered, this rested on steel uprights that moved on tracks so the entire structure could be wheeled away when not in use. Flaring out and up over the musicians like a great fan, it was made up of many diamond-shaped sections of metal, already rusted here and there. Someone had had the good sense to leave them that way, for they now looked strangely like the metal and leather shields of ancient warriors.

The audience was a difficult one to quiet down. One felt as if the music could never begin, but when it did (with the Harris) what a sound! Every instrument, all the inner voices came through so clearly and directionally that we heard notes not usually heard — a fact which much interested the musicians we talked with in the intermission. Homer Mensch, bass, and Myor Rosen, harpist, were not sure this was all good: we must be missing some of the ensemble effects (we were); or, in the words of Heinrich Keilholz, acoustics doctor to so many ailing halls, we were seeing "*through* the music." In the second part of the program no one thought about acoustics. It would be more true to say no one thought.

Mahler's single trumpet call sounded and was electrifying — echo of who knows how many other trumpets heard along that shore, interrupting the sound of the sea to announce great events or to give warning. Mahler's trumpet does both. Stately and portentous it heralds a day, or a lifetime — or is it an age? — of deadly importance in which there will be great and grave events; hearing it, one listens to the bone. And the first thing it introduces is Death — the drums of the Funeral March, deep as doom, made deeper still by the tuba's cave-dark voice, to be suddenly and unpredictably replaced by the gentlest rocking melody, tenderly sung by the horns. In places this is so quiet that tonight the sea-sound, gentled by distance, pervasive, filled in little coves of silence as it did every pause. There was no complete silence tonight, any more than there is in the blood and consciousness of living.

The second trumpet call introduces all the Furies: imprisoned anguish is given screams, grief allowed its ecstasy, twisted and tightened to the highest pitch yet also somehow transformed into — could it be beauty? — to return, even more nostalgically this time to the haunting, bittersweet rocking tune. It seems impossible to believe. Was one ever really that "young and easy under the apple boughs/About the lilting house . . ."?

The second movement, like the first, swings between lyric interludes — full of romantic surges and delays, of caressing cellos and the voice of the bass clarinet — and violent rhythms or undercurrents of rumbling strings. The cellos ruminate and ask anxious questions; the final return of the rocking melody is corrupted by whole avalanches of Furies, descending and gathering speed in nightmare rushes. After a last far trumpet call the movement ends, not with a bang or a whimper but a single muffled drumbeat on an odd unexpected note.

The sea was heard; musicians moved in their seats, adjusted instruments and turned pages; the hard-to-quiet audience was as quiet as the far-off sea. And we were in the Scherzo, rollicking in rhythm yet not really gay, haunted by a waltz as melancholy as all good waltzes are — or is it that we just can't bear much romance that real? Joseph Singer, our great horn player, played the horn solo in this movement perhaps extra *cantando* that night for the missing player in his row, a little more commanding even than that strange theme usually is.

By the time the Adagietto began the moon was very low, so near setting that its bottom tip was obscured by a tree. To the right of this an upright stone stood outlined against the sky, unilluminated. A piece of sculpture? I stared hard into the dark and made out two pale parallel verticals, a pale oval above; then it moved a trifle and I saw that it was a woman seated there alone. On the brightly lighted stage the strings sang and sighed their lament and its consolation, given depth by the harp; the conductor drew every possible tenderness out of the musicians around him. The movement seemed slower than I had yet heard it as I watched the moon touch the top of the woman's head, slip behind her shoulder. (*Je demeurais longtemps, errant dans Cesarée . . .*) Just as the violins drew the last long note of the movement out and out to silence, at that moment the moon went down behind her and sank from sight; the grieving sea took over.

She remained. Whoever she was, is, that night she was all women left with the world in ruins, mourning their dead and sick with disgust that the same drive in their men that gives them their children also kills and boasts of its killing power — its overkill — and mutilates the lovely earth with its deadly inventiveness.

But the Fifth Symphony is not all grief and suffering and nostalgia. At bright moments as peacefully gay as morning in Galilee it tells how life *could* be and in the last movement, in the coda, breaks into a surf of jubilation like that which swept over the audience when it had finished: everything now recognized, reconciled, redeemed.

Three weeks later, walking in a cozy Bavarian countryside, I told Lenny that Mahler's Fifth, as he did it, gave us life as it is and as it might be. "But that's what Mahler is all *about*," he said; then, very seriously, "Does the ending convince you?" With more hesitation than conviction I said I thought it did. "It doesn't me," he replied. "The chorale doesn't quite come off; there are all those interrupted false climaxes. I think he's whistling in the dark."

I knew he was depressed that day and this made me sad. Then he threw the end of his cigarette away and put his hands in his pockets. "Only once it convinced me," he added. "At Caesarea. I don't know why."

V

Florence

WALKING INTO THE JET that Sunday morning, the first of September, Amyas had Friday's Paris *Tribune* under his arm, bought in the Tel Aviv airport. Both of us had work to do on the flight; he handed the still folded paper over to the Bernsteins in front of us. Sometime later a terrible sound came pulsing through the roar of the jets, a sound I slowly recognized as sobbing and even more slowly placed: it was coming from Jamie in the seat in front of mine. That was how we learned about Chicago — about the defeat of McCarthy, on whom rested what hope one could find that year; for whom Felicia had worked so hard; whose campaign button Jamie wore everywhere on the tour and continued to wear with pride; worse still, we learned about the whole bloody battle of that night, inflicting even deeper and harder-to-heal wounds than those shown in the incredible photographs. Was this *America?* All three in the seats in front of us were in tears of rage and grief and stunned horror, as others behind us must have been too. At thirty-five thousand feet and roaring toward the comparative at-home-ness of

Europe, the group spirit could hardly have been lower, without comfort to give or to receive.

Crete slid away underneath, a little later the Peloponnesus; we passed over Kythera and Corfu. Someone asked me for a map of Italy — I don't remember who or why — but we began searching for landmarks and suddenly were coming down over the neat farming country circled with the shade of umbrella pines and into the airport of Rome. Buses transferred us to a special air-conditioned train waiting at a small station outside the city, at every seat a tray laid with an attractive cold lunch.

Food, at the right moment, can cause remarkable changes of mood. As we rushed through the lovely countryside north of Rome, the morning's grief was gradually replaced by hope, even an unexpected gaiety, rather like that which springs up after a funeral. Everyone grew talkative; there was a lot of visiting back and forth and, seated across the narrow aisle from one another, we and the Bernsteins tried to start a fourth political party. We finally selected Senator McGovern as our candidate. Alexander talked so eloquently about him it sounded like a nomination speech and, as his father said, if we worked twenty-four hours a day till November fifth, we could *do* it. His heart-involvement in world affairs, as always, was deep and all-absorbing; untypically for an artist he seems as world-directed as inner-directed, remaining connected to the needs of his time, and, as Richard Avedon has said of him, "working close to them, using himself completely and with a consistent sense of responsibility."

But the view through the windows also had a lot to do with that rise of spirits: it was a pastoral symphony, the image of man living in harmony with the earth. Cultivated land humped up into steep hills as it is in so much of Italy —

land looked at instead of over — has extraordinary fascination and appeal. Actual mountains with their lonely forests and cliffs are massive with secrets, but slopes of grass necklaced with vines and fountaining into fruit trees, culminating here and there in a village or an old castle against the sky, are the earth at its most fulfilled — loved and husbanded and made fruitful by man. Add to it those figures diminished by distance who are haying or cultivating or picking, children racing with a dog or herding cattle, and human life on the earth is seen in its clearest and loveliest perspective. Here in Italy, too, it was a beautiful late summer day, festive with the kind of soft white cloud we hadn't seen in Israel. Lines of poplars shimmered in a dance-in-place like that of Balinese dancers in their glistening silks; cypresses set orderly marks on random views and the cloud-dappled hills composed and recomposed themselves into delicious patterns.

Could it also be that after the jet the sensation of speed itself was a tonic? Giving us the illusion, so welcome that day, of action we couldn't take? The front car of the train had one of those glass-enclosed observation lounges where you can sit with nothing but a window between you and the track, and here many of us took turns looking out. Giddy as kids in an amusement park, David Nadien, our concertmaster, and I braced ourselves on curves, ducked at onrushing tunnels, and forgot for a while the bloodied kids in that Chicago hotel.

It was still a terribly hard day, for we had returned from Caesarea at one in the morning, done last packing before retiring, and left for the airport at eight. Immediately after we arrived in Florence there was a big press conference in a suite in the hotel. When Bernstein came in, he sat down slowly behind the green baize table and addressed the group in a very low, grave voice. He apologized at once for inaccuracies of language and asked the interviewers' indulgence. "*Sono stanco alla morte,*" he said. So was Amyas, so was I; pinwheels flared and revolved in my head. Afterwards we had barely enough energy left to call one of our daughters at home and ask if there was any fourth party movement as yet. Her husband answered; no, there was no movement he'd heard of; yes, he would keep us informed. Of Chicago he said, heavily, "It was in some ways worse than Prague. This was our own people."

Going from one country to another on the tour, even without long or arduous travel, seemed hard on everyone. All those differences that had to be digested: another language and currency, other food and customs, a changed light, an unfamiliar air. Absurd as it sounds, *we* seemed subtly changed, too, so that meeting one another in new hotel lobbies and city streets was like meeting one's family or friends after prolonged absence. It was noticeable how much more tired everyone was for having crossed national boundaries.

And Florence, after Israel, tumbled one's sense of time and history upside down; all that richness of art and the sophistication and polish left behind by the Renaissance made it feel mysteriously older instead of more recent than the Holy Land, for that concentration of treasures had absorbed events and civilizations far away in time and distance, taking from Galilee and Jerusalem, Athens, even China. Art is a greater plunderer than war used to be. And what cross-fertilizing a solitary, stay-at-home artist may be responsible for! The great patrons and collectors, whether called Medici or Berenson, gather in that honey. It tastes of everywhere.

Berenson played even further with this in his own collection at Villa "I Tatti" (where we went on our one day in Florence), setting small sculptures of Buddhistic musical angels under an Italian painting with harp-playing angels, a gracious Kwan-Yin beside a Madonna in a similar pose — making subtle use of all manner of inner connections and relationships.

At "I Tatti" I met and talked with Professor Rubinstein of London University, son of a Russian and a Hungarian, schooled in France, Switzerland, and England, his first work in Germany, married to an American and now editing the correspondence of Lorenzo de' Medici (two thousand letters actually written by Il Magnifico himself and, in Florence alone, twenty-five thousand letters *to* him). One world indeed, but much more too: a pressing down and running over, of worlds within worlds. Some times (this was one of them) it feels as if the goal of life on earth were toward constantly greater accretion of differences, meanings, and values till each original "seed" accumulates and grows into something vastly greater than itself. I have read about the inhabitants of the South Pacific Trobriand Islands, "primitive" people with ideas sharply different from ours about time and meaning. To them, the only significant history is that "which evokes the *value of the point* — or which, in repetition, swells the value of the point." It is a concept that stays with me, and one that haunted me here particularly: many lives, many deaths, creative geniuses of one period reunderstood in the light of a later one, land or city cultivated by one culture and treasured (or destroyed) by another — all build up through a combination of repetition and diversity into a coral reef of continually accumulating richness.

Now there was only time enough to verify that we were

actually in Florence, not dreaming it, to see that the Baptistry doors were safely back after the flood, the statues in their niches of the Or San Michele, to visit the seated knight and magnificent Madonna in the Medici tombs chapel. Fortunately we knew Florence quite well, so it was like looking into a familiar room in passing, but for others of the party it must have been a kind of torture. In the tangle of streets around the Duomo, crawling with five o'clock cars and crowds, we met Dr. Zea, mopping his brow, bedeviled and bewildered by the difficulties of finding one's way about. At this moment he was looking for the famous Medici chapel; he had asked people; "But they don't know anything here themselves!" he complained. We placed him on our map and faced him in the right direction and saw him off the curb — three people playing blindman's buff. A little later, while we were drinking terrible tea at a tippy little table outside a café in the Piazza della Signoria, Jack Kirkman came walking by under a clatter of pigeons, barely dodging cars and looking, with that lithe body and faun face under tousled red hair, as if he were straight out of a painting by Signorelli. Even more of the Renaissance was the expression of his North Carolina, first-time-in-Europe face: such a radiance of discovery and recognition as must often have been seen hereabout when some young Tuscan first looked at Michelangelo's David. He didn't see us behind the windblown shrubbery dividing the café crowd from the mayhem beyond but we called out and he joined us for a pot of that bitter tea, which the waiter slammed onto the table with ten paper envelopes of sugar.

If the Piazza café people are ill-mannered and crude — and I'm afraid I would be, too, in their place — the audience at that night's concert was the most elegant and cultivated

I have ever seen. And the most disciplined: not only were they deeply silent and attentive during the program, but there wasn't so much as a whisper once Harold Gomberg had sounded *A*. Such common agreement of behavior gives a sense of ease rather than restraint, allowing everyone equal access to what is being offered. It also makes, of course, for a top performance, since the artists are sustained and stimulated by it.

The Teatro Communale, in which we played, had reached its present state through a succession of changes brought about not just by choice but by World War II bombs and the 1966 flood. Its sloping auditorium floor and its terraces of well-placed boxes give a fine view *into* the orchestra on the stage, a view of more than merely the violins and cellos nearest the front edge; its white paint, accented with dark wood, and the pale coral velvet of the seats are very pleasing, as are the lights hung from the ceiling and shaded by fringed shades as if in a living room. From where we sat the acoustics were mellow and melded, the direct opposite of Caesarea, so it was surprising to hear from the musicians that for them it was not good — "The notes disappeared."

That night, after the appropriate beginning with Rossini, we heard Schuman's Third Symphony for the first time on the tour. It is a different America from Harris's which he gives us, being somehow urban and very dashing and hopeful, full of young drive and venturesomeness, as well as a kind of innocence like that of a young person first coming to the big city. In the chorale, strings, then a trumpet and a flute dream gently; the tensions feel like those of anticipation, not anguish. In the toccata a bass clarinet — quite jazzy — is a young showoff strutting among a giggle of girls who squeal and titter. Still, a drum keeps fluttering ominously and at one point a gang of young men run noisily past. Is it shots that ring out, even then, before brasses and percussion take over? One instrument after another gets its turn to exhibit what it can do. It is a great showpiece, and particularly enjoyable in a hall and from a seat where we could watch what was going on — see the woodwinds piping, heads thrown back, like shepherds in pastoral scenes, the trombones sliding in and out with the unity of a line of dancers and Joe Novotny's face lit by reflections from his giant horn like a face above sunlit water. In a box right beside the middle of the stage and about opposite the first row of woodwinds, sat Jamie and Alexander, leaning intently forward and, after the Schuman, holding their clapping hands way out as if tossing their applause into their father's upraised hands. I envied them those seats almost onstage — particularly in the *Fantastique*.

The sensational qualities of that symphony made me wonder before the tour if we wouldn't tire of it; we found instead that repetition kept illuminating the genius of the twenty-six-year-old Berlioz. Composed in 1830, the orchestration and dramatic concepts of the *Fantastique* are a full generation ahead of Wagner, seventy-five years ahead of Richard Strauss — as if its creator had acted on a dream of where music would be going. One of the earliest examples of descriptive music, a tone poem, it represents the dreams resulting from a near-fatal dose of opium taken by a disappointed lover. What is so extraordinary about the symphony (to me) is that no matter what wild and haunting things are going on, there is always a shimmer of illusion over them; some part of one's consciousness knows, exactly as it does in sleep, that this is only a dream and not the real thing. Just as well. Otherwise all those ascending and descending sizzling chromatics, the shuddering and shivering of the strings and the breathless pursuit (toward the end of the March to the

Scaffold) would be too much to bear. As it is, the demonic qualities are unmistakably those of nightmare and may be a further reason why — if you are lucky enough to be there — you are glued to watching the terrible speed of the violinists' bowing, furious as rain driven on stone, or the goings-on in the huge percussion section, where they are producing such heart-thumping effects. Then there is a great moment in the March to the Scaffold, itself the oddest combination of triumph and terror, when the cymbals instead of crashing together at a summit of sound make a wonderfully sensuous soft clash. No matter how often we heard it, I watched breathlessly each time for Walter Rosenberger to pick up the cymbals and hold them ready for that moment. It is partly surprise that takes you — the sudden restraint when exactly the opposite seems called for, partly the utter rightness at a peak of melodrama of being given instead of a bombburst the glittering hiss of a flowering rocket. And then all the kettledrums — their shiny hemispheres rich with whole continents of reflection, and Saul Goodman guiding and mastering them through thunderstorms, executions, the orgies of fiends!

One early morning in an airport somewhere, waiting for our flight, I got talking to Saul and Rosenberger and Elden Bailey, all members of the percussion section. Though I did not say this I remembered an odd piece of miscellaneous information that nervous breakdowns were more frequent among percussion players than any other musicians because of the terrific tension of waiting and counting and having to come in at exactly the right fraction of a second. What I did say was that it must be a nerve-racking and exciting business to play certain passages in the *Fantastique* (the Mahler, too, for that matter). They heartily agreed. At moments, I went on, the beat must depend on them as much as on the conductor: didn't they carry the whole weight? "Oh we have to *be* there all right — he really counts on us," said Saul. "In fact, wouldn't you agree, Walter, that we have greater potential for total disruption than anyone?"

We all laughed at the terrible idea, and Saul suddenly looked awfully pleased. As we moved toward the gate to the plane he rolled the phrase over a couple of times, enjoying it to the full.

At the end of the Berlioz, on that last huge major chord, the Maestro, who had whipped and lashed all the Furies of Hell through the Witches' Sabbath, stood with both arms upraised in triumph "like an eagle with outspread wings," as one reviewer wrote. Was the victory that of the nightmare over, or of the witches' succeeding? I was never sure. After the music and the steady rain of applause, increasing at intervals to the din of a cloudburst, the street outside was strangely quiet: just footfalls and voices and the idling motors of cars unable to move for the crowd. Where had they gone, all the frenzy and dazzling loveliness to which we had been bound? People walked along talking, back once more in the waking "real" world, which, in abrupt reversal of illusion, now felt as though it were the dream. Above the dark ridge of Bellosguardo the moon floated, higher in the sky and rounder by two days than at Caesarea; smaller, yellower moons of streetlights shone along the Arno embankment. Down in its muddy bed the river moved sluggishly, only an occasional ripple winking with moonlight. It was still less than two years since it had rampaged through the city but the only remaining sign was the high-water mark along buildings, clearly visible even at that hour and in that light.

VI

Vienna

IN JANUARY OF 1966, two and a half years ago now, Willie Weissel and his pretty dark-haired wife Carmen gave a party in their New York apartment as a sendoff to our Maestro; he was leaving at the end of the month to conduct a new production of Verdi's *Falstaff* at the State Opera in Vienna. The Austrian consul and cultural attaché and other Viennese friends were there, Felicia Bernstein, Carlos Moseley, the Philharmonic's managing director, and ourselves. Willie had gone to immense trouble to produce an advance welcome from his country. He had found an unusual old print of the Opera House, which he presented with a speech, and there were other gifts and toasts; but the high moment came with the dessert, when we were all given a confection that he had had specially designed and made in Vienna and sent over by air: white-frosted petits fours the size of a silver dollar, each with a drawing of the Opera House on it in chocolate. Lenny acted as happy as a child at his birthday party, his words rolling out in an extra-resonant voice, although over after-dinner coffee he told me that he was very anxious — frightened, really — at the prospect of what lay ahead. Conduct opera *there,* in the musical capital of the world? Of course it was an honor, but the Viennese opera audience was the most sophisticated there was and there hadn't been enough time yet to study the score as it should be studied, what with the Philharmonic's regular concerts and a Young Peoples' Concert, for which he had written the script (I knew the marathon of a day that those occasions entail, getting to the Hall at six in the morning and putting in ten hours' unbroken work, of which the actual conducting of two concerts is only a part). Well, it was the usual "time nightmare."

Hearing him talk I was reminded of another time, the first autumn of his conducting the orchestra, when he had shown similar anxiety and self-doubt. "Why do people think I'm always so sure of myself and what I'm trying to do?" he had asked me. Of course I had no answer and there was none to give. What is conducting but a supreme act of confidence and authority? Vienna, I now learned, presented a whole other and hideous dimension of *Angst* — the racial one. How would he be treated in this city that had raged with some of the worst anti-Jewish deeds of all? How would he feel there?

In scraps and bits, that February, we learned how it was going in Vienna. Willie would telephone to say he had heard from a friend just returned or had received a phone call or letter from someone there, and although at first it seemed he must be exaggerating, it grew clearer and clearer that Vienna worshiped Bernstein. When *Falstaff* opened — Italian opera based on a play by Shakespeare, produced by an Italian count and conducted by an American, the chief role sung by a German — it was such a triumph that each critic outdid the other in praise. Nor was the opera the only triumph. Bernstein also played the Mozart Concerto in B Flat, K. 450, simultaneously conducting the Vienna Philharmonic. At the end of performances the audience broke into a roar and finally, when the ovation had gone on for fifteen minutes or more, stamping and rhythmic shouts of Bern*stein!* Bern*stein!* re-echoed in the Musikverein. He was presented with the keys of the city, offered several important musical posts; there were even rumors of a movement to push him for President of the Republic.

That was 1966. In the spring of 1968 — just four months before the tour — he was over there once more, this time to conduct *Rosenkavalier*. Again before leaving, more self-doubt, more anguish, though of a new kind: yes, Vienna loved him, and *Falstaff* had been great, but *Rosenkavalier*? It was Vienna's own opera. This was going right straight into the lion's mouth. Music lovers know that not only did he come out alive but that this fresh and individual (and "unschmaltzy") interpretation had the lions eating out of his hand.

This was the city, and the musical audience, to which he was returning, with his own orchestra this time, from Florence.

Our chartered jet took off from Pisa, where Amyas and I had driven with the musicians in one of the orchestra buses. These bus rides were always a great pleasure — a sharing of anticipation and postmortems, a wonderful chance to get acquainted, and even though it was dark and rainy that morning there was the usual loud chatter and bursts of laughter and only a few hungover-looking faces in spite of the barbarously early hour. Amyas and George Feher, cellist, exchanged ideas about photography, particularly wild-flower photography, the whole way. At Pisa there were a few minutes in which to get out and gaze at the Tower and the fanciful, almost whimsical loveliness of the Piazza dei Miracoli, on which the sun, bursting out between vast continents of storm cloud, shone with sudden delicate glory.

But in the airport we bought newspapers with sinking hearts. Headlines announced that Romania, even Yugoslavia were now in danger. The jet climbed rapidly up through the cloud world and the flight plan to Vienna was told to us: over Venice and Trieste, fifty-five minutes' flying time. A few minutes later came the announcement that it was changed; we would fly over Switzerland instead, taking twenty minutes longer, and, as someone pointed out, giving Yugoslavia a wider berth.

At the airport press conference, which he took over and conducted because no one else did, Bernstein spoke (in German) of his mixed emotions on coming back this time, of the infinite sadness of Chicago and Prague. He had been horribly shaken by the occupation, so near their border, but the seriousness of the situation in the two cities was the same. Then, "You know all there is to know about me — any questions?" Yes — what had been his favorite birthday present? The answer came at once, "My orchestra singing 'Happy Birthday' — all out of tune."

The city was crowded with refugees. Twenty thousand had already arrived, and every Viennese we met seemed to have a relative or a friend whom he had taken in. The stories were heartbreaking: families split up and hunting for one another; Czechs who had been on holiday at the time of the invasion, faced with the impossible choice of returning to oppression or staying in the free world and abandoning people they loved; talented young people long ago forced into studying garage mechanics or household science now wandering in a limbo of withered incentive. Every sign in the city reading "Bratislava, 50 km." pointed like a hand of Fate, a bleak and terrifying contrast to everything else in surroundings that have over them some of the radiance and magic of a child's Christmas. Although the air was heavy with late summer, *sehr schwül,* and everyone was in summer clothes, the illusion persisted. I half expected to hear sleighbells or walk into a room in the middle of which stood a tall and perfect and very old-fashioned Christmas tree all shining with white candles. Many things combine to feed this feeling — the cozy interiors with lights glancing off crystal prisms, the incredible cakes and confections and smell of coffee, women and girls going about dressed in dirndls. I can't think why the palaces with their rows of perfectly proportioned windows, their tile roofs the rich, dark colors of crushed berries, are so pleasing to the heart unless the illustrations of childhood impressed them on us in wonderful gift books we once loved. As for the Lippizaners performing to music in their white and crystal and gold ballroom — could any spectacle be more like a spell? At any moment the proud and graceful creatures may turn into so many princes. Truly, as Lenny said of it, Vienna is a fairy story where the clocks all stopped a long time ago.

We went up to the Belvedere the morning after our arrival, and looked out over all the domes and palaces and spires to the soft, distant outline of the Vienna woods. The terrace — hot in September sunshine, already dusted with a few pale leaves — was crowded with tourists, most of them rugged-looking, simply-dressed people from countries to the east, come in big buses for a holiday tour and seeming very much out of place in that formal and elaborate magnificence. Tourists they were, not immigrants: migration continues westward, with its flow from the east dammed up, and Vienna, once the crossroads of Europe and the East, is slowly draining away, its population half of what it was in 1914. In its great years, when the Lobkowitzes and Esterhazys and Liechtensteins came to winter in their beautiful residences from the huge country estates in what are now satellite nations, they brought with them their Hungarian coachmen, their Czech cooks — many people with different traditional skills. The city's life was nourished and enriched by this influx, and when the skilled workers returned to the land after exposure to Vienna's culture they took new ideas home with them. It was all a rich cross-pollinization, based on excellence.

And now? Not only here but in the Western world as a whole? The question pressed in, insistent as the noon heat and light. Never before such vast and rapid exchange, and of what? Instantaneous images from everywhere, of crisis and disaster — and advertising. Waves of travelers: ignorant trippers, people homesick for quality wherever it is still to be found, businessmen with something to sell, leaving in their wake money and business know-how and a wealth of conveniences — miracle substances, clever contrivances, machinery for making more contrivances, bottled drinks independent of seasons or human care, television sets for advertising it all. Conveniences and time-savers, one is grateful for these, but where is there anything to feed the *senses?* Where in the oceans of technology and mediocrity in which all of us are drowning, things of quality to satisfy the heart and make one glad to be alive?

That night before the concert Amyas and I initiated a custom we practiced for the rest of the tour, of having instead of dinner a light refreshment served in our room. This first one was a poem: a tureen of fresh mushroom soup, peaches that were treasuries of ripeness, cheese, and a half bottle of wine. The table was laid with a fine damask cloth so smooth to touch it felt cool, almost wet; it was set with Hungarian crystal. The polite young waiter took time to check that everything was attractively arranged before he lighted the candles and pulled out my chair. We could hardly believe so much unaccustomed pleasure — a meal that beautifully presented, the total privacy. It was a seduction scene. Suddenly in that mellow old room in which every possibility for comfort and not just convenience had been thought of and provided, I was back in my grandparents' house where everything was a little more luxurious, there was more and better service than we had at home; back in an age when a person, with his senses and sensibilities, was more important than his money, when there was still politeness and caring: "a fairy story . . . a long time ago." In this lovely old city such things still counted, and existed; Vienna could take in and nourish the new refugees from tyranny and the continuing refugees from the world of machines. But what was she receiving in exchange?

The Musikverein was undergoing summer refurbishing; the concert took place in the Grossen Konzerthaussaal with its pilastered half dome above the stage, its very high, very ornate ceiling. The bare floor and barely padded seats made for a certain austerity and for a brilliant sound quite different from Florence so that the brasses seemed at first overloud. Whether my ears became accustomed or the musicians compensated for it I couldn't tell, but it sounded increasingly fine while remaining just as fiery.

We sat with Jamie and Alexander — Jamie's last concert,

for she was flying home next morning. She looked beautiful; her hair, usually brushed straight back and worn up on her head, hung softly around her face. Often on the tour she had been looking homesick and unhappy but now she was going home where she wanted to be and next week would celebrate her sixteenth birthday. Her profile has the special slant, the long eye of the women of ancient Crete; is it the frescoes of dancers at Knossos she reminded me of? When she turned toward me, her face, incandescent with the future and home, was that of a radiant woman; whether she knew it or not, it seemed a moment of intersection in her life.

The second half of the program began — the *Fantastique.* The strings sang their sad, haunting melody, that unrealized romance forever being interrupted or else overshadowed by the heavy entrance of brasses and sudden outbursts of the whole huge orchestra. The chromatics rushed up and down, ending at the top with a cry; after all the anguish came the hymnlike peace at the end of the first movement when the strings sound like breathed organ tones. The second movement seemed marvelously right in this setting suggestive of a royal pleasure pavilion and where the orchestra sat surrounded by dozens of stiffly pointed or spherical trees as if in a formal parterre. The waltz was at its most watery and fluid, full of waves of strong accent and the deep undulations and heartbeats of the doubled harp, the audience intensely silent (we were coming to know how many degrees of silence there are) till in the third movement the silence broke. This pastoral movement, beginning and ending with the exquisite Ranz des Vaches, is a pool of calm in the middle of all the dazzle and turmoil and heartache; it is also a few minutes of musical genius — experience translated into sound almost unbelievably whole. The lonely shepherd pipes his wistful tune (on the English horn) as if appealing for companionship; amazingly, it is answered, from very far off, by another shepherd's pipe (an offstage oboe), but tonight, in place of the magic hush, the familiar uprush of feeling "I'm not alone! A duet *is* possible!" came a sound somewhere behind us of dreadful creaking, like a ship in a heavy sea. In years of concertgoing I have experienced quite a few disturbances, including one of a woman who fainted in the front row, center aisle and was carried out like a corpse right under the conductor, who looked over his shoulder and watched without missing a beat or changing expression. Something of the sort must have happened up there in the balcony, precisely during what are probably the quietest few minutes in any symphony, though none of us dared turn and look for fear of adding to the noise. The duet between the two shepherds was taken up by the strings, affirming the delicacy and strength of communication in gentle assent — ethereal-sounding, all sky-meadows and wind, inner voices echoing the song. We were led, at the intrusion, even here, of the *idée fixe*, to the sudden tremendous agitation of the basses and plucked strings, the oboe and flute floating like two birds above them, back once more to the lonely shepherd. When he pipes his tune this time there is no reply, only thunder rolling over distant mountains; it is the essence of disappointment and loneliness. Now we would hear it undisturbed — but no, we didn't. The creaking broke out all over again, and far worse than before. Axel put his head into his hands, Jamie and Amyas and I did turn, but there was nothing to see. On those almost bare wood seats which made the slightest movement audible, a lot of people (who all seemed to be in the balcony) must have been straining to see where the second shepherd was hidden.

Happily, the incident did the concert as a whole no harm. When the symphony had swept to its wild and glorious conclusion and the long held chord had stopped, there was an uproar of applause and the entire audience rose to its feet. We had had standing ovations before, when people stood up and more and more joined them, till everyone was standing, but this was a single great surge. A moment later people began leaving their places. I watched, horrified; was it possible they were that rude in *Vienna?* Of course what they did was to pour down the aisles toward the stage, crowding just as close as they could possibly get. The musicians looked first incredulous, then more and more delighted; many had never been received like this, while the Maestro, visibly touched by this welcome back into the home of music, opened his arms as if in embrace, blew kisses, smiled through tears. It went on and on. Backstage someone laid a towel around his steaming neck and he came onstage wearing it though the audience only replied with renewed pleasure, they hadn't had nearly enough yet. At last he was driven to the little charade that never failed to work: he held out his wrist, making a show of looking at his watch, laid his head down sideways on his hands as if in sleep, took David Nadien by the wrist, and pulled him from his chair. A gust of laughter swept the hall and the applause stopped at once.

"How will you *bear* hearing the same programs over and over?" friends had asked us before we left, and we certainly had no idea then that with every concert we would hear, and discover, something new: a perfect example of repetition "swelling the value of the point." That night taught me several things. I found out how much I had counted on, and been apprehensive about, our reception here and I felt the fascination amounting almost to lust in experiencing audience response to "our" orchestra; that pleasure and deep satisfaction was one's own as part of an audience and something known objectively as well. Most of all, and because it *was* Vienna, one sensed a new cycle of enrichment. We were not just drawing on the riches of the past, we were taking a particular wealth that we had made our own, added to in our way, and were bringing it back — fresh and enhanced and vital — to its source. The rebellious youth who had stormed out of Europe to settle new land, had suffered hardship and glory, made terrible mistakes, was returning with a gift to its parents, declaring not "here I am" but "here is what I have to offer; please love it." It was possible, after all, to bring something of value to the Old World.

Next day, after Willie and Alexander had seen Jamie off to New York, we went to the Bernstein suite at the Sacher at one for a brief conference. Lenny was eating breakfast at a big table in the living room window; at a small corner desk Gretel Hilbert, widow of the head of the Opera, was making telephone calls for him; maids came in and out; twice within a few minutes bellboys knocked and came in with messages; Axel whispered something to his father and he and Jack left for a tour of the Opera House. At some point in all this, Lenny set down his coffee cup and in a kind but weary voice said, to no one and everyone, "There's too much going on at once here."

Most of the time there is too much going on at once — he draws activity to himself like a magnet. Himself? Only partly. There are times when the person, the man, seems to be looking out with an air of patient endurance from inside layers and layers of what the world clothes him with: adulation, worship, images (and reflections of images), hopes, wishes, *demands* — piled up and up, some of it unreal and based on unreal human situations. He doesn't appear deceived by the nature of this accumulation, sometimes seems entertained and stimulated by it, and undoubtedly, did it not exist, would miss it terribly. What is interesting is to see how he acts through this load, as it were, how in a roomful of people trying to meet him and get to him, ask him or tell him something, catch his attention in any of a dozen ways, he functions in a simple and direct person-to-person relationship difficult for many of us under the best of circumstances. (It would be so valuable if more and deeper study were made of the phenomenon of attention — the actual skill of an alert, flexible, and whole attentiveness, analogous, one supposes, to other skills, partly inborn but also cultivated, while the nature, or true self making use of it is the man looking out from inside all the trappings, protesting that there is too much going on . . .)

There is also, with Bernstein as with all the greatly gifted, the powerful attraction people feel to the gift itself — that mysterious flame they flutter and blunder blindly around, the fire at which each longs to warm himself. It really is a kind of fire, too. "Everyone in Vienna is a little nicer, a little friendlier when he's here," Gretel Hilbert said, and you couldn't help feeling a festive, holiday atmosphere in that suite at the Sacher, as one does even backstage in Philharmonic Hall.

So far on the tour each concert had been in a new place, but in Vienna, as in more cities to come, there were two concerts in the same hall on two successive evenings, the second one noticeably richer. For one thing, the orchestra's familiarity with the hall gave them a finer edge of assurance, and the public knew what to expect (the more avid music lovers attending for the second time) and this made for a kind of intimacy and trust that enhanced both the performance and the listening.

The second concert, Haydn and Mahler, was a great glory even though Bernstein had been heartbroken when he came onstage. It was September fifth; on the fourth, in Tel Aviv, Arab terrorists had exploded three bombs in the main bus station. What really sickened him, however, was that the Jews had run amok, beating up anyone getting off a bus who might be an Arab, rioting and destroying even in the streets of Jaffa. "I didn't know how I'd go through with the concert [he told us next day]. Then at the first downbeat of the Haydn all else was forgotten, I was in that wonderful other world."

There was an almost palpable exchange between audience and orchestra that night, one playing upon the other as the conductor played upon the glorious instrument he commanded. The exalted (and exalting) effect of Mahler's vision, translated by ensemble or solo passages of strings, winds, brass into perfect phrases — "the very phrase of angels" — belonged indeed to another world in which there were no oppressors or oppressed, no oceans of vulgarity, no hate or starvation or war. The storm clouds of tensions dissolved; conflict became concert. Yet it *was* this world: a man — and a man of severe conflict — had conceived this symphony; a man was conveying its meaning to us through the talents and devotion of a hundred others. Concert — the word, and the idea, remained suspended in the magic element into which we had all moved while sitting quietly on those hard seats that squeaked if you didn't stay perfectly still. Harmony, concord, simultaneous action, the word means all of these as well as the ineffable to which we listened: it was live proof that a great variety of individuals, using all their different skills, *can* unite in activity that is wholly beneficent, wholly beautiful.

The great symphony moved to its end, there was a heart-beat-long silence and the twenty-five hundred people in the hall broke into a roar. It was a sound unlike anything except perhaps the roar in a stadium when a touchdown is scored in the last minute of play; compared to that gale, the loudest clapping and shouts of brava are a mild breeze. How long it continued and what else occurred in that demonstration I cannot remember — only that each time Bernstein reappeared on stage, the roar broke out all over again.

By the time it finally ended Amyas had already gone backstage, and when I tried to join him a crowd of several hundred was jammed into the corridor outside the stage door. Towering above it like a lighthouse above the waves stood Ken Haas, who saw me, and with his pulling from in front and someone else of our group pushing from behind I was dragged through the resistant mass and led to the conductor's dressing room. It was a cove of quiet with the sound of the sea outside; gathered in it were such of our people as were not coping with the crowds, besides Viennese managers and friends. There was also a handful of those who seem to get into Bernstein's dressing room after any of his concerts — often people he has met the night before and been nice to, inviting them to come and see him, who linger on in the hope of being included in a post-concert party and with no sense of when to leave. Over in a corner sat the Maestro himself, stripped to the waist, leaning over while his neck and back were being pounded and kneaded by Dr. Zea. When he lifted his head he looked not only utterly drained but in a daze of nonbeing, or of being elsewhere — in what he himself calls a "no-where." If one didn't know that this happened to him, it would be quite alarming — the inner fire seems so very nearly extinguished — and Dr. Zea often did look worried, his bushy black brows going up into anxious peaks as he worked. Under his hands, however, and after several glasses of water, vitality and buoyancy slowly returned and a reviving man was telling us about the *Heurigen* where he was taking us for supper and this year's new wine.

With all those fans for him to greet, we were sent on ahead — through a waiting crowd that swirled and heaved as thick as boiling porridge and could only be negotiated by making a strong human chain — out to Grinzing and a five-hundred-year-old wine cellar where our shadows and those of monumental tuns of wine danced on the walls in the light from an open fire. Half an hour later he came down the stairs, Alexander beside him in a fold of his cape. Over tumblers of May wine and fried chicken eaten in our fingers, we heard the familiar voice and laugh ring out as strong as ever, telling stories, suggesting games; you would have thought this was the only event of his day.

The concert drew glorious reviews — one, titled "The resurrection of Mahler" being, as Lenny said delightedly, "just the kind you'd like to write yourself." He was very happy about the whole program. It was the third of our "free" days, when, having abducted him and Alexander for a few hours, we were starting out on what was supposed to be a scenic tour of the countryside outside Vienna and turned into something quite different. We had laid it all out very carefully (Lenny had done enough conducting, he said), but for some insane reason we started the circuit the opposite way from what we had planned, coming to the designated lunch place far too early and passing up altogether a famous altarpiece we wanted to see. The weather was terrible. Fog hung over the hills and it drizzled; there were no views. We seemed to be driving around and around through interminable dismal suburbs of ugly housing and uglier small industries, trying to follow a program which felt increasingly constricting and dull. When Lenny, who had been sitting cracking his knuckles, suggested that we go to the woods and find a place to *walk*, everyone's spirits revived.

Looking for the "right" place to do something, anything, is an undertaking almost surely doomed to disappointment, as anyone who has searched for a picnic spot knows. The more special you want a place to be, the more likely you are to fail, so that the best are usually found when you aren't looking at all — or looking for something else, like the way back to a parkway entrance that was missed, or a place to pull off the road and study the map. If in addition you are searching for the sake of a very special person, the wrongness of the enterprise is astronomically multiplied; in fact it is sad to contemplate how many pleasures the world's great are deprived of just because the rest of us fall over ourselves to please them. I still see in the gray mist around Vienna that day the lovely places we passed, and passed up, where paths led in from the roadside grass to the dark majesty of the forest, dwindling between tree trunks into distant perspectives, for either our young driver was trying too hard, or else he knew nothing at all about walking, for none of these places was right: we would get too muddy there, or that path led off in the wrong direction, and neither Amyas nor I had any idea where we were. But Lenny did and was soon directing him to a certain rustic restaurant in the woods where, in the thickest fog yet, our driver waved us onto a path.

View or not, what joy to be out of the car, and walking in

woods — the Vienna woods. Taking deep drafts of the fresh, loamy air we strode along, confident that the path paralleling the highway would soon curve away, uphill. It didn't. It went straight on, only a narrow band of trees between us and passing cars, a steep bank on the other side keeping the woods out of sight. Anticipation slid into disappointment, irritation, and had nearly reached despair when Lenny with a firm "it's now or never" dived into an opening in some sopping bushes and up a steep tunnel of a trail so thickly overgrown we had to bend double to get through.

It worked. We came out into the solemn silence of the great woods, stately tree trunks black with wet, a dusky half-light under the trees, and far off, at the edge of open spaces, a shimmer of spring green. Sounds here were different — smaller, lost in the multiple leaves overhead, muffled underfoot. Alexander came electrically to life. He picked out a walking stick for me, big enough for Ken Haas, and broke the side twigs off it; he ran to give me a hand at slippery places, he danced about. Lenny breathed deeper and deeper, swelling out his chest inside his white turtleneck. We were all freed.

At the top of a steep climb the trees thinned out and we emerged into a windy meadow with cows in it. It could have been the top of a mountain in the Alps where one might have heard an actual Ranz des Vaches, but there was no one at all around — not even one shepherd — and nothing moved except the quietly grazing cattle and the soft mist driving across our faces. A small house and outbuildings appeared quite deserted. Suddenly it felt like another country in which we had arrived.

New places reached on foot have a way of doing this. When you walk in unknown regions, particularly through woods or where the outcome is hidden, even more so if you have lost the way, something very strange and mysterious takes place: the hilltop or settlement — whatever it is you reach — feels utterly out of the ordinary, charged with meanings and potentialities as if it were a place in a myth. The woman who comes out of her kitchen then, rubbing her hands on her apron as she tells you the way, the dog who accompanies you for a while, the cat watching from a porch all are characters in fairy tales who may harm or help you, be sorcerers or guides from another world, or even creatures under a spell. Only strange harbors, entered from the sea, have the same magic, compared to which arriving by automobile or plane or train aren't arrivals at all.

We crossed the meadow. In the woods beyond, many trails crisscrossed one another, their signs tacked onto trees, and we stood studying them, debating which to follow. We chose one that plunged downhill but then led surprisingly away from the direction we thought it should take, certainly from the direction in which we should go. My voice sounding strange to me under the listening trees, I said we were getting lost. A laugh from Lenny, farther down the trail; "Oh-oh, think of *those* headlines!" But Alexander called back over his shoulder, "Just follow me!" Skipping and running down the slippery trail, he reached way ahead of us a meeting of paths, where a bridge crossed a deep ravine with a brook in it, and there disappeared into a mass of exotic, feathery vegetation from which at intervals his voice drifted out as if from a great distance. He might as well have entered a cave. When he rejoined us, he was carrying an armful of the most bizarre, prehistoric-looking plants with stems like miniature bamboo, each regularly circled by little cogwheels sprouting foot-long streamers from every notch. We tried twirling them and they turned into green fireworks. He darted off again and came back with two giant live snails. Overhead, here and there, leaves had faded from summer richness to faint yellow; in the quiet air, one circled reluctantly down. "Look," said Lenny, "it's already autumn," adding ruefully "and it wasn't really a summer." But Alexander, rummaging on the forest floor, came up with two small late flowers.

Back at the rustic restaurant again, for we weren't lost after all and rejoined the old path, luncheon at a bare wooden table in a low-ceilinged, beamed room was a celebration. We had a delicious beef fondu; surrounded by a sea of dishes of condiments and exotic sauces, we plunged the nuggets of beef into the boiling oil, counted out loud to keep track, experimented with different timing and combinations of dips, noisily competed and compared — all to the steady bubbling of the pot in the middle of the table between us. The skies darkened and candles were brought; we drank glasses of a beautiful Austrian "blue Burgundy," and the chef, to whom we had sent Alexander's snails, came and presented him with the shells, boiled clean. Gradually the room drained and emptied; we were the last people left. A gasp from Lenny, who I think for the first time that day looked at his watch. It was three-thirty; he had a meeting with the Mayor at the City Hall, and a ceremony of some kind, in exactly one hour!

Back once more to the world of crowds and ringing telephones, engagements to keep, people to be nice to, urgent voices saying "Mr. Bernstein, please . . ." Back once more to headlines, and war. For a few hours they had vanished: there had been air, and silence. Best of all, there had been time, time to wander and get lost, "time to look and time to care." The clocks *had* all stopped.

VII

Venice

SOMEWHERE ABOVE THE PEAKS and valleys of the Dolomites, glimpsed and lost among tearing shreds of cloud as our jet flew southward again, a conference took place between Amyas and Nick, Willie and Frank Milburn, our press representative. After much discussion two decisions were reached, barely before landing at Marco Polo Airport. One was about press conferences. Since the one in Vienna, however charmingly it turned out, had been rather a joke without either significant subject matter or direction until Bernstein took over, it was determined there were to be no more of them (with him) except for Amsterdam and Berlin; these had to be excepted since other, related occasions were involved. Instead, Amyas, with Frank Milburn to back him, would talk with reporters on arrivals and make any television appearances he could in order to spare Bernstein, for each day there were fresh examples of how his special qualities compound the demands made of any conductor on tour. Because he is so multitalented and multilingual (and enjoys picking up and using even scraps of languages unknown to him) and has the kind of presence and personality which gets the curious label of "showmanship," his arrival and presence anywhere stirred up such excitement that even more was expected of him than he already had produced. Watching from the sidelines, I was becoming appalled by the phenomenal assumption in each new city that this man could be onstage twenty hours a day — as if it were the only city he was visiting — and still conduct a great concert, still be a great musician. Were other visiting conductors led such a chase? They're going to kill him, I thought more than once with dread; this is a killing-the-goose-that-lays-the-golden-egg process. But if it was a curious way to thank him and the orchestra for what they brought, it was also the most vivid possible proof of the craving for music, and the committed artist, everywhere, the longing for a fresh wind to blow clear the sterile, violent air of our century.

The other decision grew out of Bernstein's concern for his associate conductor on the tour. Alain Lombard, conductor of the Miami Symphony, was always on call in case of emergency, attending every concert and of course being completely familiar with the repertoire. It was easy to imagine the frustration of a conductor whose hands had to stay in his pockets. Bernstein felt it was only fair to give him a chance, and good experience for him in case he ever had to take over. We were nearing the halfway mark of the five-week trip. Wouldn't it be possible, he asked, for Lombard to conduct one piece at tonight's concert? Not the *Fantastique*, of course, nor the opening number of the program — that night it was Rossini — but the Schuman, perhaps? From my seat on the other side of the aisle I could feel the rising temperature of the discussion that followed, I saw the apprehension on the dark and anxious face of our European representative,

Anatole Heller, who believed it was not fair to the audience. It was a most difficult and delicate decision, on which he was overruled, with results even he couldn't have anticipated.

The concert took place in the old opera house of La Fenice, which Amyas and I passed on our late afternoon walk. Since our last visit here the canals had filled even more with the throb of powerful motorboats and the fumes of gasoline: with eyes closed you now feel in Venice as if you were in a large city garage, so that the greatest delight is to walk in the streets. They are loud, too, but with people sounds — an obbligato of footsteps on stone over which single words and phrases or the aria sung by a canary in a cage hung outside a window are clearly audible.

Between six and seven on a warm September evening the streets could hardly have been more full — thousands of people out strolling, a few making purchases but more window-shopping and, most of all, "people-shopping." Who were all these Italians — for there were surprisingly few foreigners — were they all Venetians? They looked prosperous, relaxed, and as at ease as if they were at home; there were a great many families with small children and babies in strollers. Exuberance filled the air like a hum. In the smallest back streets the opulent festivity of Venice was exerting its force, brushing us with its seductiveness. Nowhere is one safe from it, even in the shops, since Venice, it seems, never stops celebrating — ornamenting and embellishing cloth, silver, stone, glass, whatever falls under its touch, with an overflow of abundance.

Coming out into St. Mark's Square from the close web of narrow dark lanes was like a great musical climax, every instrument *fortissimo.* Clouds of pigeons with slapping wings descended on us and banked away again; the waltz rhythms of competing orchestras beat upon our ears; gold lions grinned from tops of columns, and, ahead of us, the basilica with its softly flesh-toned marbles and exultant angels climbing to heaven was a chorus of hallelujahs. All the way out to the Grand Canal the Square was as thick with humanity as a summer meadow with grasses — murmuring, strolling, brushing past one another and gazing upward, nearly all gazing with lifted faces flushed and gilded like every other surface with the setting sun. And then we were being stunned by bells from everywhere, the nearest ones the deep bells in the Campanile directly over us, which shudder in your breastbone and set the least, most tenuous filaments of consciousness to singing. They went on and on, the deep tones reverberating, rocking back and forth in solemn, joyous splendor, rolling off every ornamented, glittering façade to plunge and strike again and again. The thrilling force of it made me wonder as I often do, at the curious absence of bells in our own country. Why do we so deprive ourselves? They give life to a city the way trees and flowers and fountains do, yet even more so for alternately coming alive and withdrawing like animate beings. And they feel like our most intimate link with the past: didn't the ears of Titian and the Doges and all the anonymous Venetians of centuries vibrate to the same pitch as ours now?

When we arrived in good time for the nine o'clock concert, the piazzetta outside La Fenice looked like an opera set designed by a genius — just the right degree and angle of lighting on the façade of the church opposite, the ideal dimness in each of the lanes, the most effective placing of the vine-covered pergola over people sitting dining at candlelit tables. On the steps and in the foyer of the opera house, people greeted one another or stood about talking, many of them beautiful and patrician-looking as certain Venetians are, the women's coiffures and clothes rather more high-style than in Florence. With some difficulty we found our seats — they were in the front of the center Royal Box. No one was on the stage yet except for Myor Rosen, almost soundlessly fingering his harp, the parterre and boxes were virtually empty. We went out again into the piazzetta. At twenty minutes past nine the musicians were in their places and two thirds of the audience, if not seated, was in the hall; this time we stayed, enjoying the exquisite baroque decor, the gilt-filigreed box fronts set with paintings, like old valentines in gold lace. At half past nine, when Alexander (who came with his father by gondola) slid into the chair beside me, David Nadien was walking onstage — even though there still were large blocks of empty seats, and every ticket sold weeks before. Alexander gazed around, at the soft old gilt, the glass, glimmery as water at sunset, the deep folds of dark red velvet curtains framing our box. He leaned toward me. "I feel like a mouse in a jewel box," he whispered. David sounded A with no effect on the ripple of conversation; Alexander's father strode onstage, acknowledged the applause, raised his baton for the Rossini. Another whisper at my side, "I hope to God I stay awake," and I thought how Axel's day, like ours, had started in Vienna at six-thirty, though while we had slept long and deeply after lunch he had spent the afternoon at the Lido and could never sleep during the daytime anyway. Once, during the Berlioz, his head lowered with a jerk, his eyes closed, and I touched him awake. It didn't happen again, though my own attention wandered for many reasons, one of them the realization that this was the next-to-last concert we would be attending together and of how much I would miss that beautiful eager face, the determined small figure hurrying through the applauding crowd at intermission and at the concert's end to get to his father's dressing room.

At the end of the Rossini, the conductor addressed his audience in Italian, making a witty and charming little speech in which he introduced his associate and explained why he was to conduct the next number. *"Aspetta sempre la mia caduta,"* he said, *"ma invece non mi ammalo,"* and waving Alain Lombard forward, he withdrew. The tall, elegant, dark-haired young man conducted well and the moderate applause he received was hardly surprising. After all, the Schuman was never very well liked over here and no one could hope to share a program equally with Bernstein. In the intermission we heard a few disgruntled comments about having been deceived, but soon we were all off and away in the hallucinatory world of the *Fantastique,* hypnotically fascinated with its frenzied *idée fixe* and shimmering visions, as dramatically involved as if it were, indeed, opera. In the ornamental boxes around us heads nodded in waltz time or leaned back dreamily against the wall, eyes closed, while many low-voiced conversations went on undisturbed by the sounds from the stage, and beneath the music there was a continuous level of sound. "You should have heard it from where *I* was," Lenny said to us later, adding that it was quite natural from an opera audience accustomed to treating music as a diversion. More than once in Italy we heard Italians tell us that as listeners they are not seriously musical people; opera, yes, and popular music — these they love — but they haven't cared particularly, so far, for the classical repertoire. Representatives of Columbia Records, men like Ernest Fleischmann, who has been a conductor himself and who met us at different points on the tour and sometimes traveled with us, were following the rising sale of classical, Bernstein-conducted recordings with an interest primed by earlier discouragement.

Fifteen hundred people heard and watched Bernstein conduct the Berlioz that night; there was a reception afterwards, for the whole orchestra and invited guests, given by the Venice festival and held in the opera house, where he was presented with commemorative gifts. Yet, on Monday, the Paris edition of the *Herald Tribune* carried the following:

> After leading the New York Philharmonic through Rossini's overture from "L'Italiana in Algeri" and William Schuman's "Symphony No. 3," Leonard Bernstein suddenly left the podium of the Venice concert hall Saturday night and Alain Lombard took over the finish of the concert by conducting Berlioz's "Symphony Fantastique." It was presumed that the conductor was taken ill, but no statement as to what happened has been issued.

And on Sunday, readers of the *New York Times* were told:

> Leonard Bernstein began conducting the New York Philharmonic at the opening of the Venice International Music Festival tonight but left the podium midway through the concert, apparently because of illness.
>
> The specific reason for his departure could not be immediately determined. Alain Lombard, Mr. Bernstein's substitute, took over and finished the concert. Neither Mr. Bernstein nor Mr. Lombard were available for comment.

None of this had appeared yet when Amyas and I set out Sunday morning for Torcello with one of the orchestra's directors who had joined the tour in Vienna. For several hours the three of us were lost to the world's noise on that tiny island where boats slide almost unheard through the twisting, grass-fringed approach to the landing and the eleventh-century basilica is still with the silence of centuries. For a while we were the only people in the church: the tall austere Madonna in her midnight-blue robes looked down from her gold mosaic heaven with oriental detachment; the peacocks in the marble altar screens turned their heads and dragged the great fans of their tails as if alone in their gardens of stone lace. The sound of our steps seemed enormous, part of a different world than this one we were in, almost a different sense. Something strange was happening to my senses, I realized, as if this whole climate of music in which we were living was growing inside me other, new perceptions — filaments of feeling able to pick up the unheard singing of mosaic or sculpture or architecture — of any design which is part of that larger order we recognize at once yet are so unable to define.

The day grew hotter, more still. We sat in the shadow of a grape arbor over the Locanda's terrace and ate local fish and drank white wine. Out in the glare, a quartet of pomegranate trees stood stopped in mid-phrase; butterflies visited borders overflowing with noisy red dahlias. We spoke of how few butterflies are left in our part of the world and wondered what they will mean to future generations when they no longer exist. Will they be all myth, then? Like unicorns?

When we had skimmed back across the glassy lagoon, the towers of Venice on the horizon as sharply clear as details in dreams, it was to find that the hotel switchboard was jammed with calls for Bernstein from as far away as Tokyo: are you all right? shall I come? what has happened? Nick Webster, trying to reassure Felicia, couldn't get through to her for the busy signals; the air was strung with inquiries, worries, theories, assurances, denials. Even now, months later, people still say to me, "Bernstein collapsed on that tour, didn't he?"

We never found out where the story came from, though I have my suspicions. Nor is this the place to comment on the decision to have Lombard conduct part of the program; like all dilemmas, this one had twin horns. The curious feature of the whole episode and of the recurrent rumors that followed it was the kernel of truth at their center, for Bernstein *had* been ill (in Brussels), his exhaustion after conducting seemed greater than usual, and at any time Lombard might have had to take over. The fiction was uncomfortably close to being fact.

The second night's concert was later in starting than the first; people were if anything noisier, yet they were tremendously enthusiastic. I wondered what a Venetian audience would make of Mahler, the world of his music being so unlike what one imagines their emotional climate to be. It was oversimple to assume that they would like him for his romanticism since he is not romantic in the accepted sense at all, and an unusually perceptive Swiss critic was to suggest the following week that Mahler has become accessible to contemporary music lovers because of Freud and surrealism and all the more daring probings and expressions of our time. "Mahler [he writes] plunged into the unconscious twenty years ahead of the surrealists; a strange sun, casting bizarre shadows, illuminates the landscape of his music."

From my seat in the curtained Royal Box, the whole delicate perfection of La Fenice seemed the second evening more than ever like that of a beautiful antique shadow box, exquisite in every detail but only a model, only the most delicious artifice. The reality was that element into which the first electrifying trumpet call and great orchestral crash plunged us and from which (speaking for myself) one is as helpless to extricate oneself as from a deeply absorbing dream. (I was beginning to understand better the dazed expression of Bernstein's face at the symphony's end). I had imagined, maybe mistakenly, that the theatricality of the Berlioz would be more appealing here, closer to the hearts and understanding of an opera-loving audience. Impossible as it is to take an accurate reading of subjective response, it seemed as though a steady development of feeling took place that night. First, people became more and more fascinated by the "incandescent passion" and "dionysian" qualities of the conducting itself; nodding in assent, exchanging glances and whispers, they showed their enthusiasm. Then, as the "mastodonic" symphony tore deeper and deeper into the emotions, mourned tenderly through the Adagietto and swept on into the final movement, I could have sworn the listeners found themselves, maybe even for the first time in their lives, in a world that is more fantastic than Venice or Berlioz or surrealism or psychedelic art just because it is stripped of all theatricality. By the concert's end the audience was totally quiet and serious, people looked transported.

The ovation over, we went out into the operatic stage of the piazzetta and the still larger stage of Venice. At the first bridge came a gondolier's weirdly called *olé* from a dark corner and then the gondola itself, small lanterns flickering at bow and stern; in the narrow lane people passed one another like shadows. The post-concert party that night was held on a hotel terrace right beside the Grand Canal — waves kissing and sucking the wall a few feet from where we sat. The moon, which had now reached the full, was already high in the sky; washed in its light and illuminated from hidden floodlights below, the white statues and great curled-up scrolls around the dome of Santa Maria della Salute glowed a delicate foam-green — all except one small pillared cupola as warmly pink as the opening of an ear.

I sat at supper between Lenny and Alexander; on Lenny's other side a lovely-looking young woman, long hair falling over heavy chandelier earrings, wearing a loosely hanging cape, or caftan, of the most sumptuous black and silver brocade. She said scarcely a word — she didn't need to, though I wanted her to have one of those ornamental nose masks on a jeweled handle which you see in paintings of *bals masqués;* it would have completed her costume. There was also a well-known and disturbingly handsome film actor, whom no one could believe I didn't recognize (they didn't know how many films I miss seeing), who talked across the table a great deal with Lenny. I turned to Axel, his eyes dark and bright in contrast to his white suit, for unlike last night he was very wide awake. We discovered our birthdays were eleven days apart and that we had been born under the same sign. We shared the same feelings about astrology, too, and he told me how promising his horoscope was; I'm going to have a *wonderful* life, he said. Turning to me, Lenny broke into a rhapsody about walking in Venice late at night: the night before, unable to let down, he had walked and walked alone — down to the Rialto and across it, into little *viali,* along *fundamenti.* That *sound,* of one's steps! There was only one other sound like it and that was a night sound, too: the hoofs of the milkman's horse in the street while it was still dark, when you lay awake as a child. And the lighting effects (he went on); you could pay the greatest stage designer in the world twenty-five thousand dollars and he could work for months and wouldn't be able to capture what just happened here. "I want Alexander to have this experience. Let's go for a walk, after this . . ."

When we went three others came too: the actor and the wordless beauty, who both entered into the night's mood, and a man who almost never closed his mouth. We are too many, Lenny murmured to me, but I knew how it is all but impossible for him to limit the swirl he starts up, consciously or unconsciously, around him. He led the way, an arm around Alexander, who walked close beside him, inside a fold of his cape. The rest of us strung along behind, singly or in changing combinations as one or another stopped to look at something, or stood and listened. It was after two o'clock, the city felt totally dead and deserted. Façades of houses and the backs of palaces shone with a blank pale glare under the moon, all their windows tightly shuttered, not a glimmer of warm light showing. In each small canal groups of shrouded gondolas, bridled together, nudged one another with soft knockings; the gondoliers, who earlier in the night dozed on their cushions while waiting for customers, had gone home to bed.

Lenny set a slow and even pace. Our footfalls rang on the stones, reflected back from walls, climbed (with a different note) over bridges, made round, hollow echoes in narrow passages — was like no other sound ever, anywhere. At a junction of two small canals, where a single lamp in an iron sconce threw a fan of light down the wall and over two crumbling steps, dimly illuminating perspectives of house-fronts divided by black water, Lenny gasped sharply, whirled himself and Axel around inside the cape, stood and stared. Even the man of incessant speech stopped talking. We entered a square with a church in it, one of those piazzas that by day would be almost solid with people and now didn't have so much as a cat to show. It was the largest, emptiest stage set we had been in so far, yet the very number of shuttered windows, the pavingstones someone took the trouble to clean, the posters on a wall all spoke of people, giving the sudden sense of people right now behind those blind walls — sleeping or trying to sleep, making love, or waiting for morning. Almost as if a wind had come up, awareness of the city's population swept over me, in a way it seldom does in cities made for cars and commerce more than human beings.

The *viale* we were on coming to an abrupt end at the Grand Canal, we tried a *passaggietta* with a long name (it was only a twenty-foot tunnel), but it too ended, in a courtyard. The Rialto, in sight now, maybe quarter of a mile away, was still complicated to reach and Amyas and I had already walked miles through the evening crowds; we said goodnight and headed home. For a few moments the sounds of the separating sets of footsteps wove a fugue, then there was nothing left but our own, louder than ever as they retraced the way we had come. We rounded a corner and two lovers approached us over an arched bridge, passed us, and went offstage into the unlit wings. On a later bridge, hands in his pockets, red head tilted back, came Jack — "Having another long look," he said. "I'm too excited to go to bed." Somewhere a clock struck three; the warm night with its undercurrent of cool air was chilling down toward dawn. In seven hours Amyas and I would be on our way north for a few days by ourselves in a small hill town near Venice, and a few hours after that all the rest would be flying off to Nice, a concert in Monte Carlo, and then two in Montreux.

VIII

Milan

UNTIL WE ARRIVED IN MILAN the following Saturday, I didn't realize how much I had missed them. Although I knew their train was not due until later, I found myself hopefully expecting familiar faces from the moment we checked in at the old Hotel Duomo, lying like a pebble alongside the cliff of the Cathedral. Amyas and I celebrated being in Milan with large plates of *risotto* at Savini's, then went off on separate errands.

Big posters outside La Scala advertised our two concerts, tonight and tomorrow, with identical programs of Rossini, Harris, and Mahler. Pasted diagonally across every poster, like the ribbons of foreign decorations, was a strip printed with the words TUTTO ESAURITO in large letters. Under a low, gray sky occasionally letting fall a few drops of rain, the people walking along the Via Manzoni looked more prosperous and fashionable even than on our last visit two years earlier, the shops had richer displays of haute couture, antiques, modern design. But it was the bookshop windows that day which attracted and held the most attention: in every one lay copies of a book about Prague — already! — open to different illustrated pages, and I joined other silent onlookers at photographs of automobiles wreathed in flames, running young people caught in mid-scream or waving fists at tanks mounting doubtful-faced, phlegmatic Soviet soldiers. No one looking at these pictures said a word; we all seemed to be caught in that paralysis which freezes people at the scene of a disaster; most, walking away, shook their heads as if trying to rid themselves of pain or restraints. Once before I had stood beside Italians in Italy looking at terrible news photographs — that time of scenes at Little Rock, Arkansas, in the fall of 1957 — and then, too, these naturally volatile, responsive people had been horrified into frozen silence. Was there never to be any end to such scenes?

By midafternoon stores opened again, the sidewalks filled, and friends began meeting at the luxurious pastry shops in the arcades of the Corso Venezia. Still no musicians' faces in the crowd. It was getting late and I was somewhere in the maze of streets east of the Duomo, yet I went the long way round to re-enter the Galleria. With every year that we are more hurried around and harried and squeezed out by tides of automobiles and trucks, this great structure becomes more of a marvel. There it stands with its two intersecting shopping piazzas ceilinged with glass a hundred feet overhead, like the nave and transepts of some gargantuan cathedral — only a cathedral to people instead of to God; to strolling, conversing, window-shopping, aperitif-drinking humanity. A great steady hum of voices rises into the glass vaulting and hovers there like bee hum in a hive; footsteps sound on the pavingstones and mosaic inlays; the air vibrates with activity that is neither hurried by onrushing traffic nor checked by changing lights. A bigger crowd by now was staring at the Prague book in Rizzoli's windows, as if at the victim of a hit-and-run driver; the fringe of tables and chairs outside cafés was steadily widening in anticipation of evening customers. Through the hum and dance, a separate sound, a single figure stood out and I heard my name and found Joe De Angelis, the orchestra's personnel manager, at a café table with a man I didn't know who looked rather like him. It was his brother, conductor of the Naples opera; they asked me to join them for a vermouth. I turned to Joe: *How had it gone?* Tremendous, especially Montreux; and he, who had bought an apartment in San Remo for his approaching retirement, was happy to have had the chance to see it again, but Monaco . . . and the Princess's reception for the orchestra . . . He shrugged his shoulders, the strong and imperturbable face came near making a grimace. The Prince and Princess came an hour and a half late to the party for the orchestra. *Why?* Because, it seemed, they had been kept waiting by our ambassador. Never mind (though obviously he did); shaking hands with a princess — and such a pretty one — had been a big experience for some of the men; one hadn't stopped talking about it since. *And Maestro?* He was tired, he looked terrible, but the concerts were great and the audiences went wild. We moved on into praise of the Galleria and *risotto alla Milanese,* which the Neapolitan brother, it seemed, knew just how to make and for which he gave me his recipe in Italian slowed down for my benefit and illustrated with lots of gestures.

We heard the concert as guests of Milanese friends in their inherited family box up in the fourth tier. "I hope I won't dishonor Il Presidente by having a little nap during the Mahler," our host had written in his letter. Instead, and in spite of almost insupportable heat, he grew wider and wider awake as the great work unfolded, and at the concert's end looked as astonished as if it were his first symphony. We had heard the Mahler now in Ghent, Jerusalem, and Caesarea, in Vienna and Venice, and in each place it had sounded different. Once again it was new, sounding extra-rich, I supposed, partly because of all the associations of La Scala itself. "Something of all the great performances here must stay behind," as one of our musicians said afterwards, and each one we spoke with had loved and been inspired by the realization of where he was playing. Still, it must be more than that; the sound was so enveloping, it had such resonance in one's head and nerves that it seemed at times to be originating there. And then it was explained to us: the wood in the walls of an opera house or concert hall becomes seasoned, is actually changed by the music itself, just like the wood of a great violin.

The concert over, we moved on to a large and formal reception at the Continentale, to the special table where every placecard but Amyas's and mine had contrived names — R. W. Emerson, D. Alighieri, J. G. Whittier, L. Garibaldi, L. Boston (!) — in an attempt to discourage impersonal strangers and save room for such friends as "Mr. Boston" himself might collect and bring along with him. Our hosts and conspirators in each city were kind and sympathetic to this plan but I was always terrified that a reporter might discover us and ruin the whole game. Tonight there was only one, very special, guest: "Wally" Toscanini, the great Maestro's handsome and vital daughter, with her father's strong eyebrows and piercing look, a rich voice and sense of humor. Seated between us, she and Lenny fell into a torrent of reminiscences and jokes, Amyas and I protecting them as best we could from the self-important intruders, sincere admirers, autograph and publicity hunters — each of whom almost invariably disclosed his intentions before a word was spoken. Sometimes Amyas and I exchanged messages with our eyes: are we dragons? bookends? what are we doing here anyway? maybe we should leave . . .

We walked back to our hotel together with Lenny and Willie, in a misty dampness smelling of the wet pavements and the glossy cobblestones bright with reflections. Lenny suddenly remembered a time he had been here in Milan a few years ago when Callas, scheduled to sing Medea, had some infection which prevented her singing but not being about, and Visconti had an entire extra month in which to perfect the production. The three of them visited costume warehouses together, spent two hours, he said, examining just *buttons.* Think of it! Then another three hours going over *feathers.* Describing it, he walked slower and slower, till the four of us were standing there in the empty Via Manzoni, he with his cape flung back, sketching out the entire scene.

On past La Scala, all locked up now and dark. Once more he stopped, in front of one of the posters with TUTTO ESAURITO plastered across it. At the far end of the building, Biffi's restaurant was still open, small groups sitting over late supper. Perhaps it was the sight of this quite ordinary activity virtually denied him in his unordinary position that made something inside him snap, with an almost audible twang. Whatever it was, it catapulted him into a passionate, despairing outburst against the demands and pressures of being on tour, of being constantly on show, almost never having time for such a thing as supper with a friend at some pleasant restaurant — no leeway, no pause for rest, no time to spare.

We listened, helpless, heartsick, already deeply concerned as we were by his exhaustion and the way he looked. Outside the door of his suite, when he had said goodnight and gone in, the three of us turned to each other. *No more* formal receptions, we said, except certain embassy ones that can't be skipped and unless he really wants to go; we'll have to do the best we can without him; this can't go on. Getting ready for bed with heavy hearts, Amyas and I admitted miserably to one another that Bernstein, and therefore the whole tour, seemed on the brink of collapse. And it was by far the hardest part that lay ahead, with ten concerts in twelve days — and six of them in Germany, I said to myself.

Rain fell steadily all next day, building up from time to time into noisy downpours. Water standing in the piazza in front of the Duomo bounced upward under each of these onslaughts and cloudbursts drove pedestrians into subway entrances and herded them into tight huddles on the Duomo steps. All the way around the huge building the gargoyles spouted magnificently, water flew in fine spray off the hundreds of stone angels and saints, the innumerable knobby spires, and flowed in rippling sheets over the vast slopes of roof. Lenny, who had a cold, stayed in his suite with its view of his favorite gargoyle, and finally got some rest. A few blocks away Wally Toscanini held open house, receiving the many members of the orchestra who came to call and to look with veneration at mementos of her father with which the house is filled. Night came early, and with it the second successive Mahler.

W had finally succeeded in giving us seats where I had been longing to have them — close to and beside the stage. In fact we were virtually on it, being just inside the stage entrance in a room about nine feet square known as the stage box. A narrow bench ran along the upstage wall and against this we pressed ourselves as flat as we could to give more room to the artists passing through and, during the performance, to be as much out of sight of the audience as possible. We were there early. Many of the musicians walked past, greeting us; Nick and Ken and Joe came in and out, looked at their watches, conferred; we met La Scala's managers. Then came David Nadien, slender and polished like the Guarneri violin under his arm, and *A* sounded and swelled as all the strings joined in. A long pause, a long silence; heads and eyes around us stayed turned toward the inner door of the box, expectant. Always that pause was agonizing. If it felt longer than usual I had to forcibly crowd down the images of fear and sit on the lid, and tonight it was much longer. Was he ill? Had the cold been the last straw? Nick and Ken's calm seemed exasperating. Finally I breathed easily again: the distinctively deliberate footsteps approached and the Maestro came through the small door in full stride, in full command, looking collected and focused. There was a slight but perceptible check of surprise, a flash of communication when he saw us there, and then he was out in the downpour of light and applause and the concert began.

We weren't listening to the music, then, we were *in* it, part of it — so tremendous and extraordinary a sensation I could only imagine it like being in the center of a beautiful storm, swirling around us, sweeping us on with its great momentum, relentless, charged with movement and power and subtlety. The sheer din was unbelievable. Twelve feet from the thunder and lightning of the percussion section, I was staring at the back of Saul Goodman in the circle of his kettledrums, a box of sixteen different drumsticks at his side. Sometimes his actions were as rapid and dexterous as a conjuror's as he tuned, leaned over to listen, seized sticks and beat drums, laid them down and seized others, putting in perhaps one accent, then retuning and listening. To our right, the bows of the first violins drove like gale-slanted rain out of a single cloud, or sighed as in a single breath; their unity, like that one singing voice of the horns and the velvet of the trombones, animated by the Maestro's fantastic dynamism, was all but unbearably overwhelming. Though I was outwardly still — I had to be, where we were sitting — my heart was leaping with excitement, inside I was singing, dancing, whirled and tossed as if sensation and emotion would burst the skin of my being.

Around us in the little room an almost continual excitement and anticipation and participation accompanied what was happening out on the stage. After the Overture and the Harris, Jack was there with a towel, a glass of water, and a lighted cigarette for the Maestro's comfort between curtain calls; various managers stood waiting and watching — always at the ready. Over and over I saw La Scala officials exchange looks of amazed admiration and nod, smiling with pleasure, and all the while, on stage, the huge, live creation raced and charged along or dallied playfully, whispered or stormed. Sometimes we were in the middle of an August thunderstorm, at others beside a quiet-running brook or drifting among sunset clouds that gently divided to disclose widening lakes and fjords of light; or we were in a gale at sea between thundering canvas and the roar of wind and waves or in a preview of Judgment Day in which the angels' praising was ripped across by screeching fiends, yet all, all of it under control, ordered, held in perfect and inevitable-feeling balance.

What a creation a great symphony is! What an activity! For which Bernstein's hyper-aliveness seemed a fitting match; it must take that kind and degree of aliveness to bring score, instruments, and players into a dynamic whole: Mahler and he and a hundred and six artists created the storm together.

Sometimes during a concert it can be fascinating to detach yourself from listening: stop following the music (though not to drift on one's thought) and try becoming as aware of what's going on there onstage as if you knew nothing whatever about musical instruments or the music they play—were a visitor from another planet where no such thing existed. There, in quiet and orderly rows, over a hundred men and women are sitting or standing, holding curiously shaped boxes of highly polished wood strung with twisted wire and the internal membranes of cats which they brush with hairs from horses' tails; or blowing into huge convolutions of brass as elaborately twisted up as intestines; or beating on covered bowls and rows of pipes and smashing metal disks together; and so on. The imaginativeness of it honestly rivals such inventions of nature as the cricket's scraping his legs together.

But those instruments, fanciful and whimsical, perfect and logical as they turn out to be, are only the beginning, when you realize that the sound they make together holds two or three thousand people immovable in their seats, quickens pulses and brings tears, sets them to clapping and shouting and stamping and (rarely) even to roaring, while no words or pictures or anything but music itself can convey the release of the heart, the visions and the intimations of Reality it gives. This *is* life, you feel, if only for a flash; and just as in certain dreams, or when you have been under anesthesia, the Answer is all there and is perfectly simple and you want to weep for the indivisible is-ness of everything — even the horrors none of us can bear — so, in whatever place you happen to be in in your own life, you hear as you once heard in childhood and as if from divine authority: IT IS ALL ALL RIGHT.

And what about the musical notation, the score? By what extraordinary genius, chance, evolution, did people — not like you and me, agreed, but nevertheless members of the same species — key in to those elegant mathematical laws of the universe which determine such matters as major and minor modes, tonic and dominant, and like a boy on a fine windy day fly the kite of their musical ideas on their frail (comparatively) line, into those upper gales?

So very very few things which men make, and call creations, are really that, even when made by artists or dreamed up by inventors. They are new and imaginative combinations of already existing substances, usually representing or suggesting something else which has also been there before. And maybe it would be brighter of us to recognize this, to admit that for all our inventiveness and imagination *no one* creates except Nature, or God, or Brahma. If we saw that, we might perhaps stop applying that beautiful word "creative" to selling hosiery or bonds and pause before destroying the creative balance of nature or such of its creations as trees, and whales, and birds . . .

Yet somehow, with music, man's inventiveness and imagination did go beyond combining and copying. Working with natural laws and using their beautiful infallibility and rightness as a sail or kite or airplane wing uses the air, imagination went on to create what had never been before. Or nearly: birds make melodies and there are birds (in Africa) that even harmonize with each other — on a couple of chords. But a whole symphony? It is not, thank God, Prometheus' fire, but it certainly partakes of what feels like divine mysteries and magic, which even musicians can't penetrate. "What *is* it, with music?" I once heard Bernstein say to a friend, and they shook their heads and laughed.

And, carried along on the river of it that night, watching it being made by all the companions of our journey, I thought how an orchestra, even when it's not playing but is just traveling, and being, is like some enormous organism engaged in its own intrinsic patterns of activity, being attended to by its helpers, guided and steered.

Halfway through the Mahler the baton flew from the conductor's hand, though almost before it dived among the second violins another was handed to him. Then, somewhere in the last movement this one, too, took off and there was a second replacement. The going seemed heavy. What whipped up that beautiful storm for the rest of us was, we learned later, a nightmare for the conductor that night. The Mahler seemed endless, he said; the heat was terrific and he was so wet he had soaked one handkerchief through wiping his face, looked for a dry one and couldn't find it right away, was swimming in sweat and couldn't see, had a coughing fit, needed five hands instead of two. *I was under water!* he exclaimed, seeming to relish the frightfulness of it in the telling.

Walking home through the Galleria, at that hour empty of tables and chairs and people except for a tight circle of our men bursting with merriment over a magnificent joke (to judge from the laughter echoing in the cavernous glass), Willie told us that Lenny was, right now, having supper at Savini's with a friend; he had arranged to have the restaurant kept open for them. We smiled at one another, and strolled on into the outer arcade to show W the ammonites in the pavement. He had never seen them, didn't know about them, but there they are, embedded in the stone outside the shops selling gloves and ties and turtlenecks: the curled-up shells of snail-beings who inched blindly after food on the ocean floor more than a hundred million years ago.

IX

Munich—Bonn

THE NEW YORK PHILHARMONIC had played in Munich only once since the days of Hitler and World War II, and had never played in Bonn. More than half of the orchestra's personnel is Jewish. How many of these men's relatives and friends had been persecuted, or wiped out? "They gave flowers to Mr. Bernstein today," first violist Lincer told the press in Bonn, "and twenty-five years ago they probably killed fifty of his relatives." Some of our men had last been there as soldiers with the Allied Forces. "I can see from here," another violist, Leonard Davis, told a reporter, "the site of the pontoon bridge across the Rhine I helped guard . . . it's weird." Violinist Borodkin, whom one always located at once onstage by the shining mass of his white hair, had, in Germany, the one deep wish to get over into East Berlin and visit his father's grave; he wanted to take a photograph of it for his mother. Highly charged memories and feelings and impressions must have imbued, and, who knows, perhaps even sent out unheard signals from, the planeload of souls taking off from Malpensa that Monday morning for Munich.

The flight was barely that — just a spiral climbing and climbing over the same flat fields and tile-red, splatter-shaped towns in order to gain altitude, a few minutes over the cloud-floor concealing the Alps, and then a reverse spiral on the other side, this time over evergreen forest, lakes, and fields that were brilliant viridian even on a cloudy day. Forty-five minutes from the closing of the door in Italy to unfastening seatbelts in Bavaria.

The crowd waiting for the plane to roll to a stop was as bright as a bouquet; light sparkled on the mouth of a trumpet, a horn. We were being met by a brass band. Out on the ground, dirndl-clad girls presented me with armfuls of flowers as was to happen at every stop in Germany; with Felicia not there, I was the orchestra's first lady. I can't remember what the band played, but they were wonderful to watch with their befeathered hats and lederhosen and one trumpet player whose face blew up dark red when he blew and deflated to normal skin color when he didn't — a red balloon in reverse. They clamored for Bernstein to lead them, which of course he declined to do, later expressing his annoyance to us in the car on the way into town, for either you have to act the clown in such a situation (he said) or you appear grumpy. He was neither on that drive. He was flooded with terrible memories, memories of conducting a totally ex-Nazi orchestra in 1948 "who somersaulted from all-out contempt of me to hand-licking, in half of one rehearsal." Of conducting the Dachau orchestra, "what remained of it — seventeen musicians, the wind players too debilitated to have enough breath so we had to keep stopping for rests." His eyes were full of tears. The green fields brushed past.

Forty-five minutes in the air, perhaps twice that on the

ground, and we had moved from the high-ceilinged, tall-windowed, often dilapidated buildings of Italy, tight-shuttered against sun, to blocks of houses bright and neat as those of toy villages, set with as many shining small panes of glass as possible to let in the sun and stormwindows to keep out the cold; changed from dark, shiny-eyed expressiveness to fair-skinned efficiency and reserve. On a table in our room lunch for two was laid: the beer so exactly the right temperature someone must have been standing outside the door and rushed in with it at a signal, the eight or nine kinds of sausage and cold cuts decorative and artificial-looking as that plaster, dollhouse ham which the mouse Hunca Munca attacked in a fury in Beatrix Potter's *Tale of Two Bad Mice.* We could hardly dent it either, there was so much, but a slatternly maid who was writing letters behind the door of a brightly lighted cupboard in the hall answered my request to remove the tray with a cold stare, and when we had gone out drank up the beer we didn't, and left the remains of the meal on the floor outside our door.

No concert that night; the evening was memorable because of friends. In each city remarkable individuals stood out among the hundreds, maybe thousands we met — such people as the Verhaegens and Teddy Kollek and our driver Joseph and Ben Joseph at Ein Gev; several who entertained us in Vienna (like the young waiter in the hotel); by now a whole host of them, with different backgrounds and languages and looks and points of view. Yet they had something in common, which even in a very short time and in such unlikely circumstances as crowded receptions, made itself felt, something whose delicate but strong filaments were becoming woven by sheer multiplication into one fabric, a tissue of faith. Immediate humanness, you might call it — the sensitivity to feel and the ability to meet another at his point of reality, where he really lives; "blood-relations of the mind," the poet Ruth Pitter calls those whom one feels that way about, though, analyze it as best you can, it remains a mystery.

That evening it was Margot Hielscher who entertained us, whom Lenny had met in 1948, a film and television actress of mature beauty and enveloping charm. Finding Amyas and me waiting in the hotel lobby she took a chance and introduced herself, having hoped when she saw us (she said) that we were the friends Lenny had asked her to include. Her eyes, like her mouth, were wide and generous; she was wearing a black-vested Bavarian suit with a white ruffled jabot. Lenny, joining us, took one look and said she was the perfect Octavian — why hadn't she been there for *Rosenkavalier*? Accompanied by Jack, more shining even than in the Piazza della Signoria or on that midnight bridge, we headed out on foot into the town, the restored old town with leaning gables and leaded windowpanes and Gothic-lettered signs hanging out from their poles like banners, past the Hofbräu Haus (where it all began, Lenny murmured sadly, an appalled look on his face) to the Haxenbauer restaurant Margot had selected for dinner. It was a hot, smoky, cozy, bare dark wood place. Margot's husband Friedrich was already there, blond and solidly built, with a scar on one cheek — an insatiable music lover (we learned) and an occasional composer. Dinner matched the surroundings: wonderful mild white radishes large as beets, cut into paper-thin spirals and eaten with black rye bread; pork hocks (for which the restaurant was named) so crisp-skinned you couldn't hear for the crackle of your chewing, and, of course, Munich beer; all accompanied by much mellow-voiced, humorous storytelling of Margot's and joking of Lenny's. We were all very merry, we felt very close.

Ten minutes away by car, in a garden beside the Isar, was our hosts' house, where we went later and were joined by Friedrich, who, Margot explained, always bicycled instead of going by car. We were about a dozen in the big studio living room, where a fire burned and dogs walked in and out, and a little peasant maid out of an operetta brought trays of cheeses and we drank tumblers of a very light white wine. Lenny talked long and earnestly with the distinguished journalist "Sybille" — and Amyas found a film actor and his wife whom he liked very much. There was another journalist, introduced simply as "Hunter," and the actor Gert Fröbe ("Goldfinger"), a great redheaded man who would be clumsy if he weren't graceful, and famous in Germany less for his films than for his extraordinary miming. Someone said he was even better than Marceau.

It was good to see Lenny, who had only one other evening left when he wouldn't be conducting, so relaxed and easy, and once, when all other conversation stopped, to hear him talk freely and colorfully about a popular musical he was asked about, the gist of it being that he found it very vulgar and therefore dull, using a vulgar word to describe it. Fröbe, meanwhile, had been telling me about his particular, and one imagines unique, specialty in acting: a miming of poems. He illustrated with one about a candle flame being blown out, vanishing in smoke, saying, "I'm only one small about-to-be extinguished flame, but I AM FIRE! If I could just reach that curtain, that closet, I could kindle the house, the village, the world!" And he began to act. The large hands traced the fine swirls of smoke, he made you see the subsiding flame and the spark, then nothing. "I *am* the flame, you see, when I act this!" he said. And he was, and it was curiously moving. When we left around one o'clock, the party was still in full swing.

It was Margot who made much of the next day delightful as well. She joined us and the young Lombards for lunch at a fine restaurant to which Friedrich, however, wouldn't come; it was too conventional for him, she explained, reminding us that he bicycled instead of driving a car, "once he even bicycled all the way to Salzburg." Her tales of his passion for listening to favorite recordings, over and over till three A.M. — so that she bought him earphones, which of course fell off when he went to sleep, releasing a blast of sound that woke them both up — were full of wit. They may also have been a kind of solace, I felt, to the young assistant conductor's wife, who, I suspected, was suffering from a surfeit of music. Margot took us, too, to the Royal Cuvier theater — that baroque rhapsody to joy, followed by a stop for a glass of wine with Friedrich in the old palace guardroom, now a *Weinstube* filled at that time of day with plain people dropping in from their jobs and sitting at long bare wooden tables. I found Friedrich — quiet, eccentric, scarred — rather endearing.

What stood out about the concert that night, what I remember best about it, was the intensity with which Gert Fröbe, very conspicuous in the front row of a balcony to the side of the theater, followed it, a rare intensity almost equal to that of the conducting. And then at supper afterwards, the scion of an ancient princely house and a Hapsburg archduchess — one of the few Hapsburgs left — were still other threads in a huge tapestry whose pattern, if only one could get farther away from it (or have clearer sight), might possibly become discernible. Accretion, "swelling the value of the point." History here seemed as thick-layered and, yes, as bizarre as certain aspects of the city itself in which I had wandered about by myself during the morning while Amyas was taping an interview for television. Medieval city, perfectly restored after the Nazis had been burned out; a modern subway now tunneling away underneath it (and, above, the usual boardings plastered here too with posters of a violent sadistic-looking movie); the exquisite taste of the royal Residenz and the lovely innocence of diminutive dirndls I bought for new granddaughters; and, all the time, hovering everywhere like an unmoving and immovable incubus and in spite of warm, wonderful individuals, the awareness of Dachau, fifteen miles out of town in those green, green fields.

I suppose we all experience times when the script writer really outdoes himself, convincing us that it, or something very like it, actually exists. And if it doesn't necessarily stick to the unities of Time and Place, how it hammers away at unity of Action, taking fiendish delight (so it feels) in putting in a bit of black humor here, a fine streak of irony there, at all times operating with a masterly sense of balance, an audacity of plan beyond that of the greatest artist. There are other days with less dramatic unity, perhaps, but with too many coincidences and inner connections for any logical explanation; somebody, somewhere, must be pulling strings. Or it could be that the "play" is always that full of conjuror's tricks, only sometimes a layer of insensibility is removed, making one more than usually aware of every least resonance and echo and sign.

The day I'm coming to began for us with a time discrepancy: the bus left a half hour earlier than we had expected.

We made it, but only after a wild scramble, full of irritation, and Amyas, hunting for socks, saying (in a voice very sharp for him) that some one of these mornings he just might find he'd packed his *pants*. It sounded rather like a challenge.

At the airport, Dr. Zea looked as harassed as though he had lost his medical bag; his eyebrows were up on end. I asked him if he had enjoyed Munich. "I didn't have time to see anything of Munich," he protested. "I kept thinking I'd see this or that tomorrow but — TOMORROW IS YESTERDAY!" Ah yes, Paul Zea, and not only that September.

A face floated up out of the crowd, a large figure, overcoat flapping, approached with agility through the crisscross of hurrying humanity: Gert Fröbe, round-faced and eager, on his way to Rome to make a new film. There was much well-wishing and gratitude and *auf Wiedersehens*. He was dear and I was sorry to see him vanish again through one of the airport gates, sorry to be leaving behind Margot, and Friedrich with his bicycle and his passion for music — is there anything that twists the heart quite like the finding and at once losing again of what feels like one's own?

Walking out to the plane, Lenny asked me if I had seen the article about him, not a review but a column done by that journalist who had been at Margot's house, the man called "Hunter." No? He would translate it for me. Sitting beside him on the flight I listened to his reading of the text at the same time following it myself, though intermittently distracted by the almost grotesque photograph which leered slyly in midpage. The caption beneath it read: " 'Exploded' at cocktails: Leonard Bernstein." The headline: "Bernstein Scolds and Swears."

"Seeing him sitting relaxed on the couch, slippers up on the table, one might take him [the commentary began] for

The start of the tour. (Left to right: Ralph Backlund, Department of State; Frank O'Connor, President of the New York City Council; Mrs. Charles C. Tillinghast, Jr.; Charles C. Tillinghast, Jr., President of Trans World Airlines; Leonard Bernstein; Jamie Bernstein; Amyas Ames; Evelyn Ames; Alexander Bernstein)

". . . trunks and trunks of violins"

". . . and glistening horns."

". . . all that breath and intensity converges and focuses."
(Harold Gomberg, oboist)

Engelbert Brenner practicing the Ranz des Vaches,
Joseph Zizza holding the score.

". . . the guest of honor . . . sat between his two children."

"Archways and lintels of huge stones . . . shone in the illumination."
(Caesarea)

". . . a fact that much interested the musicians we talked with in the intermission."
(Caesarea)

". . . gilt-filigreed box fronts set with paintings,
like old valentines in gold lace."
(La Fenice, Venice)

"... there was a reception afterwards"

". . . for the whole orchestra."
(Venice)

Managing. (Left to right: Nick Webster, Willie Weissel, Frank Milburn)

"And then in midthought, in midpain, we had landed."
(Bonn)

"On TV, live . . . bathed in brilliance
. . . the music of Berlioz's opium dream."

"While Bernstein autographed for a crowd of two thousand."

". . . a deep sense of gratitude and communion welled up."
(Berlin)

a baseball coach, for a manufacturer of sporting goods, a fashion designer or ex-track star with the look of a playboy," and continued in the same tone to tell everything "Lennie" had said at Margot's, to call his expressions of opinion "explosion of temperament," to fasten on that one vulgar word he had used (far worse in German) and repeat it over and over (which he hadn't).

"Naturally [wrote Hunter] on the question of musicals, Bernstein is somewhat embarrassed. The worldwide popularity of *West Side Story* must surely make it hard for him to comprehend [the new musical's] following . . . Is the Maestro already too old to discern the new signs on Broadway?"

Hardly a sentence failed to be equally carefully crafted and sharpened and dipped in venom to bring down its prey. It could serve as a model of how to demean and diminish.

I felt as if a stone had lodged in my stomach. What a betrayal. Of Lenny, first, but also of last night's intimate group and of that home itself. But "Hunter" was one of the guests! . . . I tried to shake away the inevitable sequence of thought, yet remembered how another prominent friend had once been maliciously led to talk at a small party only to find it all over a national magazine the next week.

The subject, and object, of the piece was less angry than depressed, disheartened, and, most of all, troubled by this image the world had of him, deploring "this 'Lenny' business" from a perfect stranger. I couldn't tell him, not having read it yet, what Richard Avedon wrote about this. "That a man of Leonard Bernstein's quality [it reads] is so often called Lenny by his detractors indicates that he has not been cautious, that he has been trusting, accessible, remained vulnerable and left available in and to himself what lesser men, out of fear, cut off." But I tried to analyze the reasons for such curious attacks, for the apparently irrational criticisms leveled at the greatly gifted or extremely prominent, which in his case, I feel convinced, are a reaction to his hyper-aliveness that the less alive feel as an affront.

It was a sad talk we had. Although he seemed less exhausted and had come noticeably up from Milan's depths, he was more anguished than ever by world tensions and without any hope for their resolution. The personal attack on him was just another small part of man's warfare on man.

And then in midthought, in midpain, we had landed and were on the ground and out among the photographers and cameras, the extended hands and bouquets, and a young woman in costume was offering something to him — a mammoth sparkling glass full of Rhine wine, a loving cup. He drank from it and it was passed around and someone was saying to Amyas that the press conference would be up on the second floor of the terminal building, please come this way, and a man I hadn't met was saying to me that I had an appointment at the coiffeur's at two-thirty, here was the address (handing me a card). Was some kind soul here that thoughtful? or was my hair that awful-looking? I never saw this stranger again. If it hadn't been that there really was an appointment I might have dreamed him.

Lenny and Jack, Nick and Willie and Zea — all the rest melted away, as people do in dreams — and I was now in an upstairs room with long bare tables and straight chairs and filing cabinets, trying to answer the somewhat difficult questions put to me by two reporters from London (what were *they* doing here?) while Amyas was getting seated by the microphones. "Right after this," said Frank Milburn, "we'll be going to Bonn." I realized I had no idea where we were.

"Where is this?" I asked. "Cologne." Though of course we weren't even in Cologne but in a nowhere somewhere, though a rather pretty one of more very green fields neatly bordered with evergreens.

On the drive to Bonn, Frank blew up about Hunter's piece — Frank, who is gentle and reasonable and whom I had never seen worked up over anything, was red-faced with fury. My own grew along with his. What was worse, the ghosts of horrors I thought long buried came and stared once more, hollow-eyed and dying, out of the past. In front of me, the neck of our driver, so silent and correct, filled me with misery and suspicion: was this man understanding everything we were saying? Would he report it all to the press? Was he the *enemy?* I hated the way I was working inside. Poison from the dart of hate was breeding more poison.

At the hotel ("you'll love it, it's right on the Rhine") Lenny and I resumed our interrupted talk, he sitting, somewhat slumped, in an armchair before a wide window. Behind him flowed the Rhine, swirling crossriver traffic tail-to, sweeping barges downstream at incredible speed, and raising thick-churned waves in front of those going up. Along the embankment right outside the hotel, three sightseeing boats — *Brünnhilde, Siegfried,* and *Beethoven* — lay tied up, waiting for passengers.

It grew very dark in the afternoon and began to rain; still many of our group went to visit the Beethoven house or took river excursions. I slept, and on waking studied the guest list for the night's reception. Place: the Embassy Club at Bad Godesberg. Hosts: Ambassador Henry Cabot Lodge and his wife, "in honor of Leonard Bernstein"; immediately following his name, those of every member of the orchestra and the instrument he or she played. Only after Joseph Zizza (assistant librarian) came the names of ambassadors, cabinet ministers, the Lord Mayor of Bonn, and all the distinguished guests who were expected to attend, altogether three hundred and sixty-six names.

The Beethovensaal, close to the river and only recently finished, made use of tested traditions as well as innovations. Its asymmetry, and the ceiling, which looks like crumpled-up yellow paper, seemed at first glance self-conscious, even contrived, but the use of wood, the generous stage, and wonderful lighting everywhere soon offset that impression. From the first notes of the Haydn the sound was very beautiful — as though the hall had no need of associations or thousands of performances but was seasoned and mellow and ripe from its conception.

Almost at once the sense of *concert* that night was unusually strong, though it is not easy to understand how one felt this, even less to account for it. Perhaps it was the audience, probably the most international of any we had had, or the mood of the musicians, who had all received the same guest list that we did and therefore knew they were to be in fact guests of honor at an important reception; whatever the reasons, a special harmony of participation surrounded and maybe even inspired the music. Watching Bernstein lose himself and become the music he conducted, the morning's sadness and bitterness dwindled and receded: the universe we were being led to apprehend had its own solutions for animosity, malice, evil. If only we could become more aware of them, learn to trust them — in my Father's house are many mansions . . .

The Ranz des Vaches in the Berlioz was its most poetic and delicate, seducing me to listen as if survival itself depended on each thin sweet note. We had talked in some airport or hotel lobby recently with Engelbert Brenner, the English horn player who at the end of the movement pipes without reply, finally fading away into soundlessness and solitude. His face, like Harold Gomberg's in oboe solos, turned bright red with the effort; how (I asked him) did he reduce the sound to the point he did? He admitted it was a chancy business, for if he should ever reduce it by a fraction too much nothing would happen, and no sound at all would come out; that was his nightmare. Each playing of it (he went on) was a fresh contest with Bernstein, who kept luring him into playing softer and still softer — "He plays with me like a cat with a mouse, you know" — while he, Brenner, watched the conductor with such attention that some of his colleagues kidded him about his beginning to look like a Jew.

We were marched to the Scaffold then, and at the death-blow all fantasy stopped, the head rolled away. In the Witches' Sabbath, the grotesqueries and nerve-twitching effects seemed as natural and effortless tonight as though all Bernstein had to do was draw them out of the air with his baton. On to the last great chord and his arms stretched wide in triumph. The nightmare was over. In the seat beside us, a critic whipped out his notebook and wrote something furiously, said goodnight, and hurried off. Outside the hall, among the headlights and creeping automobiles and long brocade dresses held up off wet gravel, someone said, "That's One World for you — French music, conducted by an American Jewish composer, in Bonn."

At the reception, which for all its size was personal and beautiful and warm, with flowers and decorations arranged by Mrs. Lodge herself, we received with our hosts and heard the guest of honor tell them how marvelous he found the

Beethovensaal. He *floated* on the music, he said; it was like being on a cloud, he could have conducted all night. And he looked it — face smoothed, eyes calm and content. But as soon as he had had a drink and met some of the notables he went to sit with the Ambassador and talked seriously with him about Germany, and Berlin, and the world.

All around us, conversing with the musicians, were diplomats, German and American officials, citizens of Bonn, even a royal princess. In front of every window, ten-foot-high standards fountained at the top into white candles and white and yellow flowers; against the walls, the leaves of live aspens and willows stirred and trembled in the warm air: there was a continual glimmer and movement and murmur as rich and hypnotic as summer afternoons. One of the violinists, kissing my hand, thanked me for sitting beside him on the bus that morning. (This morning? Munich? That was days ago!) Engelbert Brenner came through the line and whispered, "I played tonight for *you*" (or did I just imagine he said that?). Willie, looking drawn around the eyes, said, "I was so tired this morning I found I'd packed both my shirt and my socks." He laughed and moved on, but it was Amyas I heard saying, "Some one of these mornings I just might find I have packed my pants."

Back at the hotel between one and two o'clock, he was handed a telegram: WATCHED YOUR TELEVISION INTERVIEW TONIGHT GREATLY IMPRESSED AND WE ARE VOTING FOR YOU TO BE NEXT PRESIDENT OF THE USA LOVE YOURS MARGOT FRIEDRICH HELEN. Did Munich always have to have clouds over its name?

In the upstairs hall, framed in a doorway against a theatrical-looking bluish background, Jack, in his shirtsleeves, was setting one of the Maestro's big suitcases outside the door.

When Amyas remarked on his working late, Jack shrugged ever so slightly, then beamed and said, "Wasn't it a *beautiful* party?"

On the table in our room lay a postcard, most recent in an amusing series sent us to every city by a son and daughter-in-law who were also in Europe, moving around us in a different order and itinerary. We picked it up and read, "Hope Bonn is bonne, you're having fun, Munich no pain. Want to do it *again?*"

I went to the window. The river was still alive with traffic — red and green port and starboard lights, masthead lights, lit-up windows of barge cabins. Rain danced on the esplanade and doubled the lights where *Siegfried, Brünnhilde,* and *Beethoven* waited, tied up and still, for morning. "A Day in the Life," I thought, falling asleep, and still think of it by that name.

X

The Castle

I HAVE JUST LOOKED IT UP once more, in an even bigger atlas; I still can't find it. I know that it ought to be, was, and presumably still is, about fifteen miles northwest of Frankfurt am Main but at that point the map stares back, blank, very pale blue. Of course it is the town I looked for — the castle would hardly show — and I'm sure there was a small town right beyond the big gates of the park. After all, the castle had to be somewhere . . . or did it? For it wasn't even an *echt* castle but a nineteenth-century copy of one with the moat only suggested, the tower — and in fact the whole Schloss — with more and larger windows than it should have had, and many *gemütlich* features no real castle ever had, such as a porte-cochere and a row of the coziest bay windows, one of which was in our own room.

We appeared to be the only guests — Lenny and Jack and Zea, Willie and the two of us — though I distinctly remember other very much alive people: an unusually helpful young man who seemed in charge everywhere, whether at Reception or running the one tiny lift or answering the telephone; two waiters — one Ethiopian, the other Egyptian — both equally beautiful; and, less prominent although there in a silent chorus, several other people (also young) waiting around in the courtyard to catch a glimpse of their hero. And although we never saw him and only sent him messages, there was the chef who sent up for our supper small artichoke hearts in a sour cream and dill sauce and an unforgettable clear soup and for Lenny's a bisque of crayfish, flown from Turkey, and half of a roast partridge. That chef was a poet. There was also, in the rose garden beyond an artificial grotto, a very old gardener tying up roses with raffia, who pointed out to Amyas and me the way to a little willow gate and a path we were looking for.

Getting to the castle was unrelated to anything else. The entire morning — sulphurous and rain-drenched, with the Rhine still throbbing to that vast, continuous traffic — went into conferences and telephone calls to the embassy about the safety and advisability of Bernstein's attending an opera in East Berlin the day after tomorrow; it couldn't have been more pertinent, or more pressing. Then, once Amyas and Zea and I stepped into a car and drove away, we moved right out of the ordinary world and if that was still there, we were as unaware of it as the snorkeler is of the airy world right over his head.

It had stopped raining, though as so often happens after summer rain, the air was more saturated with moisture than ever so that everything looked as if seen through gauze. We drove up the Rhine. Long, heavily loaded barges — very medieval-looking, with banners at the bow and canvas tents like huge pavilions over their cargo — swept by unheard or passed behind islands. Drachenfels and the Venusberg with their castles, other castles and ruins, vineyards and great trees appeared dimly in a mysterious light and dissolved again; one wasn't even wholly sure one *had* seen them. The only big city we saw, it was Coblenz, I think, was barely a mirage in the clouds. Across the river and up a long grade through rich, dark forest we saw that the speedometer needle stayed at an even one hundred and forty kilometers an hour; our driver entered, left, and switched autobahns with great skill in order to give us (as he said) the most interesting drive. He did; we saw a lot and all the while Zea, who was seldom free of responsibility this long, chattered away about his boyhood and about the difficulty of staying near his boss as he was supposed to do ("why I can't get even into his *neighborhood*") and about Berlioz; now there was a screwball. In Monaco (he told us) there's a statue of him, and after the concert that night there were our boys, looking up at him and giving him hell and shouting abuse at him. They'd all had a few and here was their chance.

We drove over what seemed a kind of pass in the Westerwalde; we saw a crazy village of half-timbered old wrecks of houses leaning drunkenly together in a huddle at the top of a pinnacle; we went down a long incline. Though I couldn't understand everything our driver said, he seemed to be telling us we were near the Schloss, and something else I couldn't catch, for I was distracted by unmistakably seeing — over a low wall and in a big meadow with trees in it, moving peacefully along in the deep grass — a small herd of African gazelles and four zebras. A few minutes later we drove in through the castle gates.

When the helpful young man had left us in our room we broke out laughing: where *was* this? and *what* was it? The room might have been in a great-aunt's house in New England — brass bedsteads, faded watercolor paintings around the fireplace — all of it. Let's go for a walk, we said, which is how we came upon the old gardener. You must go through a small gate (the helpful young man again, talking) and then you will be on the path that circles the park. Only please be careful, don't go off the path onto the lawns, it's dangerous. How could it be, I asked Amyas as we crossed the would-be moat, but he had seen what I hadn't: it was a golf course.

We saw no players; standing all around the course and here and there on the incredibly green fairways, monumental specimen trees pointed up and disappeared into a soft mist. No one, not the manager or the Egyptian or Ethiopian waiter or any of our party, knew what kind of trees they were; to me they looked rather like sequoia and redwood and cedars of Lebanon. At the foot of one right beside the path stood a toadstool almost big enough to seat a small child under; under another, an outsized Albrecht Dürer hare, with eyes like big drops of dark liquid about to fall from its head, kept us in sight for a long time, his sides blowing in and out with fear before he loped away across the grass.

Of course it was dark when we were driven to the concert so there was no chance to see then, either, where the Schloss was; blindfolded and turned around three times (as it were), we were sent out into the night and, twenty-five minutes later, drove up to an immense silvery dome, resting like a brilliant half bubble on the dark ground. Around it seemed to be a park of some kind, or a mall with fountains, and around that the rows and rows of rectangular blue-white illumination of factory windows. These were the buildings of the famous Farben Industrie; the concert was in the Jahrhunderthalle, or Centenary Hall, built to honor that occasion.

Inside as well as out it was spectacular: huge open spaces

uninterrupted by any supports and a kind of lighting in which tiny human figures — dark, scissor-shaped, or wearing evening dresses to the floor — looked like the brushed-in figures in architectural renderings. Not until they came close and you saw eyes and mouth and heard voices were you quite sure they were alive and real. The auditorium floor was flat, without any slope; where the side seats ended there were no walls, no aisles or boxes — just space. The single, very large balcony looked as if it might be moved, or enlarged, or even removed.

We were on TV, live, during the *Fantastique*. The illumination was intense, hot white like a star, the televising itself more subtle than is customary. Snouts of carefully hidden cameras poked out from holes here and there — moray eels in a coral reef; other cameras were large Cyclops eyes; occasionally a human hand or forehead was briefly and partially seen behind these — eyes behind eyes, mind guiding senseless no-mind. Bathed in brilliance, aimed at from all directions, the conductor dreamed the music of Berlioz's opium dream into action for the musicians to play, while all the tubes, carefully sighted as guns, received the music and the image of its making, to be translated and given out again all over Germany.

When we were shown into the conductor's enormous, day-bright dressing room after it was all over, he raised his head and stared at us. "What — you at *another* Berlioz? Why don't you kids go to a movie just once — there are good ones around. Tomorrow, now . . . no, not tomorrow — that's the Concertgebouw." He seemed pleased just the same and insisted on coming to the reception, particularly, I think, because he wanted to talk with our fine consul in nearby Frankfurt, where so many Americans were stationed.

The castle, when we returned to it, loomed huge and insubstantial in the mist, which was much thicker here than in the factory-land we came from. Whatever our location, it must have been at an altitude of one or two thousand feet and we were in a cloud; the air smelled of mountain forest. "Let's walk out a few minutes," said Lenny, turning abruptly away from the massive, many-windowed shape.

With him leading me by the hand we set confidently out along what felt like a path under huge trees, the darkness so thick it was another element. From beside us came cracklings and rustlings, the mutterings of Amyas and W, thrashing around in search of a way through to the open fairway. Was there a way through? We kept meeting a wire fence and a ditch; I walked straight and full into a wide, springy bush that let half its leaves full of water down on me. Yet somehow, and with Lenny leading bravely, we found an opening into the vast dim space between the trees. Their lofty, silent presences, at different distances and degrees of substantiality, looked like an old-fashioned stage set seen through a thin curtain. The air was soft and moist; the light, filtered through mist, silvery. Lenny groaned with delight, striding along in his great cape across the drenched turf, taking huge deep breaths.

Let's dance, he said, when we were well out in the middle of the misty moonglow. We joined hands and, with him singing and directing, did an absurd minuet: out, arms extended; in to the middle, bowing; clockwise around and kick; counterclockwise, the same. Only he was any good at it; Amyas and W and I were terrible. We wandered on, skipping and floating in a world where we felt without either weight or substance. A large, pale crescent showed in the darker grass and, nearer, became a sand trap. "Look at it," said Lenny scornfully (he loathes golf), "that's what I spend half my life in — sand traps." On the far side of it an invisible downward slope gave our bodies a forward lean, our knees a ridiculous lightness. We joined hands and took off, running till we had to stop for breath.

" 'Yet mark those trees two miles away/All clustered in a clump,' " Lenny said, surprisingly, and something — could it be? — about a pig who couldn't jump. What — we didn't know Lewis Carroll's "Pig-Tale"?

> "There was a Pig that sat alone
>   Beside a ruined Pump:
> By day and night he made his moan —
> It would have stirred a heart of stone
> To see him wring his hoofs and groan,
>   Because he could not jump."

More stanzas of delicious nonsense followed — one in which a camel hears the shout and demands to know "Oh, is it Grief, or it is Gout?/What is this bellowing about?" and one in which a frog — "a sleek and shining lump," volunteers to teach the Pig to jump. Now our actor's voice took on richer emphasis, a still slower and more dramatic pace:

> "Uprose that Pig, and rushed, full whack,
>   Against the ruined Pump:
> Rolled over like an empty sack,
> And settled down upon his back,
> While all his bones at once went 'Crack!'
>   It was a fatal jump."

Outburst of merriment, absurd sense of release. Running downhill again with joined hands we snapped the whip with each end man in turn. The dew flew up against my legs in a cool spray.

Meanwhile, "those trees, two miles away, all clustered in a clump," were growing larger, became towering sorcerers in peaked hats, melancholy madwomen in hoods and veils, reaching out arms in wide medieval sleeves, pale ghosts peering over the shoulders of those in front with more and still paler ghosts behind. Not entirely pretending, we stopped and gave them a kind of shuddering bow before wheeling around and returning toward the Schloss.

Partway back the Pig-Tale was resumed, this time its opening and closing choruses:

"Little birds are dining
  Warily and well
  Hid in mossy cell:
Hid, I say, by waiters
Gorgeous in their gaiters —
  I've a Tale to tell.

How are we going to find the way through again? Just look at those *trees!*" Lenny interrupted himself. They were indeed mossy cells; no sign of an opening anywhere. Under them once more, our sight vanished; we moved ahead by testing and feeling. In the darkness the voice went on, unhesitating, as the astonishing memory unreeled:

"Little birds are writing
  Interesting books,
  To be read by cooks:
Read, I say, not roasted —
Letterpress, when toasted,
  Loses its good looks."

Leaves rustled underfoot, we went down into the same ditch and out again.

"Wonderful effect he gets with that rhyme scheme . . . Know what it is?" I was asked unexpectedly, but Lewis Carroll, and the test, were made to wait, for in whatever direction we now moved we came up against fencing. More crashing around and exclaimings, then a prolonged clatter of wood as a board at the top of the fence fell off. We climbed over and under its wires, waded into what felt like softest, ankle-deep mud but — to judge from my shoes when I finally saw them again by daylight — was grass-cuttings, and so returned to the original "path."

By this time the little birds were tasting "Gratitude and gold,/Pale with sudden cold/Pale, I say, and wrinkled — / When the bells have tinkled,/And the Tale is told." The curious sadness at the heart of high comedy seeped through the lines like the mist through the trees.

Well, that tale might be told, but another was about to unfold for back at the edge of the court in front of the castle, our leader charged up a grassy bank facing the entrance, planted the long fence pole he had brought along with him like a spear in the ground, and in a great voice proclaimed:

"You know, we French stormed Ratisbon:
A mile or so away
On a little mound, Napoleon
Stood on our storming-day . . .

Let's storm the castle, men!" he shouted, aimed the spear at the massive walls, and lunged forward. Amyas and Willie, as buckled with laughter as they might have been under pounds of armor, stood at his side, ready for the assault. The deeply resonant voice, at full volume now, declaimed:

"Once more unto the breach, dear friends, once more;
Or close the wall up with our English dead!
In peace there's nothing so becomes a man
As modest stillness and humility:
But when the blast of war blows in our ears,
Then imitate the action of the tiger;
Stiffen the sinews, summon up the blood,
Disguise fair nature with hard-favour'd rage . . ."

And now in the drama I found myself in the role of helpless maiden held as hostage and was down on my knees, wringing my hands and imploring the conqueror's protection. Peeking up shyly from where I knelt under rolling waves of poetry, I looked straight at the figure, bending close above me and dark against the sky, of a naked bronze man — a discobolus — almost at the same instant that the end of the spear struck it with a ringing clang. The surf of poetry broke into horrified gasps, laughter, worried speculation and fears we had done damage. W was at once the self-collected, charmingly helpful Willie again. "Don't give it a *thought,* Lenny. It will be on the bill in the morning."

But the castle — where were the lights that should have gone on, the windows thrown open, and angry voices shouting at us to keep quiet? Nothing at all happened. To the end the castle remained as unreal and unlived-in-appearing as if it had been in a tapestry forest, though when we entered the hall, blinking, there was the helpful young man to greet us and send the Ethiopian waiter (or maybe it was the Egyptian) for the drink the Maestro had not yet had.

XI

Amsterdam

THE PACE OF THE DAY, beginning dimly and slowly, steadily accelerated. The tempo of the whole tour was steadily accelerating, as perceptibly as music approaching the end of an *allegro* last movement of a symphony. Like the sonata form, too, themes that had already been experienced and developed, seemed to reappear vividly a last time with, just before the coda, a stretch of comparative calm in which everything slowed down before the *prestissimo* finish.

There were very few hours for sleep after taking the castle — only three or four for its conqueror — for we had to leave for the Frankfurt airport at nine and the musicians, who were scattered about in various places as far away as Wiesbaden, must have started even earlier. Driving away from the Schloss, there was just time to notice that a long thin board was leaning incongruously against the shoulder of a bronze discus-thrower before castle, court, and statue dissolved in mist. Somewhere in a suitcase emerald-green slivers were still glued to a pair of evening slippers; there hadn't been a moment to remove them.

Fog delayed the plane's departure for Amsterdam and, perversely, on the one occasion when there was a pressure of events on arrival: Bernstein was to receive the Edison Award for the year's distinguished recordings at a ceremony at the Concertgebouw and after that would hold a TV interview. He took a moment as he always did on the plane's landing to say goodbye to each member of the plane's crew and autograph the programs and record jackets held out to him, but once inside the terminal was rushed through the crowd and into a waiting car. There was a police escort, a white-helmeted creature who swooped and banked on his motorcycle like a skier on a mountain, coolly turning to look at us over his shoulder to make sure we were following. I smiled inwardly at the fun of it and at the absurdity of human nature (at least my own) for taking pleasure in a situation which if I were on the other side of it, driving a car or walking along on my own business, would produce such different feelings.

Every seat of the chamber music hall at the Concertgebouw was filled with an audience awaiting our arrival for the ceremonies to begin. Heads turned at our entrance, doors closed behind, and the speeches and awards at once began. Bernstein's came last, to the most applause, acknowledged by him in two or three minutes of quiet eloquence. We were just leaving at the ceremony's conclusion when we saw that there was to be a recital: a group of musicians came onstage carrying recorders, a small organ that was set on a table, a viola da gamba and some extremely odd, attenuated horns that looked as if they belonged on the heads of a particularly exotic species of gazelle; they were krummhorns, I was told. Though interviewers and cameramen were waiting in the main auditorium, Bernstein begged to delay proceedings, and we stood by the door and listened for ten minutes or so of purest, other-world enchantment. It was personal, intimate music of a kind friends might make together, added to in one number by two singers; the mood was reflective or stately, or else gay with the sort of innocent mirth the world seems to have utterly lost. Hearing it in the daily stream of our magnificent orchestral music surprised the ear, and the heart, in the same way Shakespeare's lyrics do in the headlong surge of his drama.

The taped interview, of which I shall say more later, was carefully staged and the replies of a kind that take the concentration and timing and alertness of any performing art — surely that was enough for the first half of the day? No, there was still more to come before anything like a hotel room or lunch could be considered. On to another room, circular and echoing with a din of voices, crammed with newsmen and photographers clambering over furniture and over one another like ants after dropped food to get to the man they had come to see. Questioners' voices drowned in the cacophony; even the answerer's, which only a few hours ago had resounded against castle walls, could scarcely be heard. I noticed with distinct relief the width and solidity of the table behind which he and Amyas sat, for the fifty or sixty men and women of different ages and appearances all had that voraciousness of the "media" which is like that of hounds around a surrounded fox. And what was it really about — this pushing and shouting and slavering for a few photographs, a few lines in the newspapers? Man's hunger for celebrities? for music? Or the hunger for the artist himself in a world of machinery, the craving for that person, man or woman, who speaks with feeling directly to our own feelings, inciting love, not hate?

A voice made itself heard. "Mr. Bernstein! You have said

you will compose after leaving the orchestra. Is that all? What, would you say, are your *goals?*"

The room grew less noisy at that; Mr. Bernstein glanced down at the glass of orange juice in front of him, giving it a few turns before he answered. By now there was silence.

"That would take an hour — at least — to answer." Pause. Smile. "But in a word, it's *communication,* I guess. Whether in conducting, or composing, or explicating, I want as much as possible to communicate music, which is, I suppose you could say, the one language we all have in common."

Instant release from the tension of close listening; a kind of sigh of recognition.

This century's hungry heart, self-exiled from nature and God, and magic, tearing itself to pieces with hate and protest and then offered as food a better car or refrigerator or more exciting vacation, is starved for "passion carried into it alive" for the reconciling and *connecting* of art. If music is the one language we have in common, what it tells us heals division and makes us, for a little while, whole.

In our honor, the music-loving Dutch had banked the stage front of the Concertgebouw for its entire length, with chrysanthemums and dahlias and asters, so high the violinists and cellists were hidden to their waists, so deep it looked like a garden border. All through the concert the blooms under the podium trembled and danced; the floor, at the evening's end, was sprinkled with petals.

It is a hall magnificent for listening, overornate and rather ugly by present standards but, like La Scala, so surrounding you with sound the music might be coming from inside your own head. The orchestra loved playing there. The audience loved them. The moment the conductor appeared in the doorway at the top of the long flight of stairs leading down to the stage, everyone rose to his feet; even at intermission he was given a standing ovation.

The music that night was more than music — it was an element in which we lived as long as it lasted. It sustained, surrounded and carried us on its motion, at the same time that it abstracted and distilled the essence of reality. Of all the arts, the philosopher Alan Watts has said, "music is the art most like reality" — that unseen reality behind appearances. This mystery was almost translated for us into visible and physical as well as auditory language. All of it was on television, live. Millions watched and listened.

We felt very gay in Amsterdam; meeting one another around the city, the smiles and expressions of ease and relief were noticeable. No one wanted to leave; don't you wish we could just *stay* here? was the greeting one kept hearing. Though Lenny and W left early the morning after the concert in order to attend the new Felsenstein production of *Traviata* in East Berlin, the rest of us had a whole free day — an airy, early autumn day it was, with a high bright sky and huge soft clouds sailing up from over the housetops and spires, with more following as soon as one lot had floated by. Everything was in motion. Wind, rushing up and down along the canals, rustled the trees and tossed leaves away, raked the water up, streamed the laundry drying on houseboats out horizontally or made shaking fat men out of shirts and pants. Even the thousands of windowpanes, going bright and dark with every change of light, seemed from any distance to wink and dance.

Like many members of the orchestra, we took a sightseeing tour through the canals and out into the harbor and we walked, a game full of challenge here since the embankments don't always lead to bridges where you expect to find them and there you are, waves slapping the wall at your feet and the row of houses opposite staring across a dance of water. Yet the canals and the sky — so much of it, in Holland — are both freeing and connecting in their effect, the houses facing one another across water not nearly so separated from each other as houses divided by glaciers of traffic, while always, somewhere near, there's a footbridge to take you across. I find something heroic and lovable about a people which fights the ocean back with dikes and then turns about and uses waterways with intelligence and respect.

Almost at closing time we found the flea market, where tired salespeople and elderly customers come in from the country were standing about eating raw herring dipped in fresh-cut onion, while girls in gaudy miniskirts and their shaggy-haired young men were still rummaging through piles of old velvet and beads and fur out of a hundred attics and the valuable displays of antique brass and Delft china were being packed up hopefully for another day. We went back to our hotel for tea with a remarkable woman whom a mutual friend had asked to call. The Baroness von Till, honorary *dame d'honneur* of the Court, now an ardent painter, bird lover, and conservationist, had a Frans Hals vividness of coloring and expression. As she talked with us and invited us to come to visit her in the spring she radiated vitality and hopefulness; not till the very end of the visit did it come out (and by chance) that she had spent four years as a prisoner of the Japanese in a concentration camp in Java. "Oh I learned a lot there," she said, adding — what was the precise adjective? — "people are fantastic."

I had heard my missionary uncle speak like that about the Chinese and their habit of leaving girl babies in park refuse boxes, with an almost amused astonishment at the Creator's whimsicality. At home again, the mutual friend told us the Baroness had been tortured; her hands still bore horrible scars.

No one wanted to leave Amsterdam. I stood for a long minute in the door of our corner room on a canal, looking back with affection at its fullness of light, the windows filled with sky and clouds and gulls, at eye level, racing downwind. On the center table stood a pot of African violets a friend had given us, highlighted as if by Vermeer, and each sharp yellow eye glowing like a small sun. Finding the young Spanish chambermaid in a hall linen closet, I tried to explain the flowers were for her to keep, but she didn't understand and our car was held at the door while the messages flew that the lady had left something behind. The lady had indeed — but it wasn't violets.

XII

Berlin

WHEN WE CLIMBED INTO THE SKY from Schiphol airport, the musical instruments, which had traveled all over the Continent in trucks, were right with us in the belly of the plane. I had watched the trucks draw up outside the Concertgebouw the day we arrived in Amsterdam — three of them, huge and yellow, "New York Philharmonic Tour of Europe" painted on their sides in blue letters two feet high; they were coming in from Frankfurt, or rather Hoechst (that silver-bubble hall), having traveled all night.

"That's the last time we'll see *them,*" said Willie, standing beside me. "From now on the instruments fly." He was very crisp about it; his mouth looked tight. Why? I asked. "Because we don't dare drive them into Berlin, they might get held up at the border or detained in some way . . . too risky." In the forward hurl of days and concerts and countries, I'd forgotten about Berlin and the diabolically intricate geography of its approaches. So there they were, in all their special padding and trunks, loaded and stored with the help of our own three baggage masters, and I was reminded of the look on one of the musicians' faces when he said how exciting he found it leaving home: "that big jet taking off, with all those beautiful, precious instruments aboard."

The departure from Amsterdam and then the flight were dislocated and troublesome. A car ordered to take us and a director and his wife to the airport failed to appear, so we went late, by taxi. None of us felt well; Sam and Miriam had colds, we had dined too well the night before with our young lions and were no longer accustomed to that meal anyway; the cab had derelict old springs and stank of cigar. In the airport, Jack Fishberg, violinist, always jovial and courteous and ready with a story, met us with a face of stone: his mother was critically ill and he was flying home. And finally someone had left a suitcase in town so that the plane, fully loaded, sat waiting on the apron with Ken, on the ground, alternately looking at his watch and at the gate through which at last a young man shot out, bag in hand.

We were barely in the blue when the captain addressed us: we would fly twenty minutes out toward Hamburg at our present altitude, then (he was sorry) he would have to descend to ten thousand feet in order to enter the Corridor to Berlin. One has read all about this; it's quite another matter to experience it — one of those truisms which if they weren't true just might make history so different. What obsession for revenge, or power, what egotistical webspinning or Satanic stupidity blocked the air — *air!* — for a hundred miles around a great city, necessitating three corridors, each only ten miles wide, through which planes must fly at easily observable and therefore uncomfortable altitudes?

It was a dark gray day with boiling clouds and such turbulence at ten thousand feet we flew the whole way with seatbelts fastened. The Captain, misjudging a tail wind, was ahead of Estimated Time of Arrival and suddenly announced we were landing, while directly under us a forest of high-rise apartment buildings grew in our path and didn't stop or ravel out into fields but went hideously on and on as if we were over Brooklyn without Kennedy or World Fair Grounds or Rockaways or any clear space whatever; and just when the whole prospect seemed utterly impossible, a runway opened up right between buildings and we were down on it, hurled against seatbelts by the thrust of reversing jets. "United States Air Force Base," a sign reads, "Tempelhof Field"; the buildings are all army-drab. Helicopters with a white star on their sides squatted here and there like gigantic mosquitoes; Jeeps with soldiers in them scuttled about. Yet even in the rain, and with no Bernstein aboard, there were warm and friendly welcomes, flowers heaped in my arms and Willie, with a hug, the first to reach us.

Much of West Berlin and all we saw now is commercial and up-to-date, monotonous as many parts of New York or any big American city; our hotel room — utterly functional and without charm — was similar to, even if better than hotel rooms at home. Oh, what we had left! I stood at the wide picture window and looked out at gray miles of buildings under a gray sky, all of them the same height and no variation in the height of the land under them. To one side of the hotel, passing almost under us and stretching off into unseen distance, ran the double tracks of the rapid-transit "S" *Bahn.* Trains were rushing back and forth, unheard because of the window's insulation; I might have been watching an old silent black-and-white movie. Unreasonably exhausted I lay down to rest, not bothering to draw the curtains, it was so dark, when across the window-framed sky flew a huge bird with slow powerful wingbeats and majesty of purpose, blindingly white against the dirty clouds: a single swan. I was awake, not dreaming; it seemed a kind of omen.

Tickets for our three concerts had gone on sale in Berlin on a Sunday four weeks earlier. Five days before that, on the Tuesday, people began waiting in line, having friends bring them food or getting replacements, even camping out when necessary — but waiting. Every seat for the three successive evenings was sold. We were very curious about the hall, particularly since Bonn, when I commented on the daring effects of the Beethovensaal and was told "wait till you see Berlin." Planned as part of a complex of buildings not yet erected, it looked from the outside like a child's cardboard construction with one side caving in; but inside one stepped into a bright fantasy of wide halls at many levels, connected by flights and flights of airy-looking stairs and lit by festive hanging globes, while one surprising circular stairway spiraled upward among all the angles and straight lines like the open core of a shell. Inside the auditorium, the audience is separated into many groups by steps, balconies, exits; the floors have a dihedral slant like airplane wings — mildly upsetting at first, since one is forever treading changing gradients, but very effective in removing you a little from the usual and the expected. Unexpectedly too, the stage juts out into the audience and has three large banks of seats around it as well as those "out front." We sat in one of these, right over the double basses and almost facing the conductor; people farther to our right were looking right at him.

I wished we could have photographed them. Young people, probably music students and young musicians, they all leaned forward at one angle of intense absorption, blond heads shining in the brightness streaming down on them from above. A bed of Darwin tulips can look like that in mid-May, all the stems at exactly the same slant, heads neat and compact and expectant. The view into the front rows of audience behind the conductor was a sad contrast. Some, I'm afraid our compatriots, were quite openly asleep; one pretty woman wore an unswervingly sweet smile as if she were in a receiving line at a debutante ball. With *that* music! With all our inmost terrors and griefs and joys being gone through for us by conductor and orchestra, purging the emotions as Greek drama used to do — though perhaps even at Delphi and Epidaurus somnolent fat men dozed through *Oedipus,* the hetaera beside them beaming with the sheer enchantment of attending the play. I am being too harsh.

It was a very majestic, unusually tragic Mahler we were given that night, though somewhere at the very bottom, and out of an ultimate dark oceans below what seemed to be darkest, new hope was dredged up: mind and heart, grown accustomed to feeling, not seeing, were given a fresh kind of sight, a new organ of perception. After all those hearings, there were still new things to hear. Perhaps because of its gravity, the work felt slower than other evenings. It was, in fact, only twenty-nine seconds longer.

The next day, while Bernstein autographed for a crowd of two thousand people, Amyas and I went over into East Berlin. "Over," one says, as though it were situated a few hundred miles, or a range of mountains or an ocean away. It is farther than any of these.

Willie, bringing us up to date the day we arrived (as if weeks had passed since we parted in Amsterdam and not twenty-four hours) told us about his and Lenny's going over, for *Traviata.* They had gone by subway, Lenny insisting they do it just like anyone else, and it had taken forty-five minutes to get through the border: the numbers of every

Express cheque had been taken, they stood in line, cash was listed and changed and so forth. As for crossing Checkpoint Charlie late at night (for they were driven home), under the searchlights and guns, it was sinister, ghastly, *ghastly!* His attack on the word sounded like a bone cracking. You're exaggerating, Willie, I thought. He wasn't.

If you don't look around too carefully, it is rather like any frontier, with conspicuously striped gates and men in uniform moving about, each one presumably with a home and family somewhere, and an innocuous, temporary building, too small for what goes on in it and rather dingy, where people wait, and wait, warming themselves on a chilly day at portable heaters, sitting on wicker furniture beginning to resemble a field of winter stubble, waiting and listening to the worse-than-a-dripping-faucet sound of unseen typewriters painstakingly, slowly — how slowly — clacking out those facts about a person which matter the very least, yet just because they conceivably might be his one Ariadne thread back, or the noose around his neck, are all set down. Passports are slid through a slot and a tiny receipt pushed back; the passport is eventually returned, the receipt taken. On, then, to the next gate.

Only the waiting rooms are like a million million others. Between them and between gates stretches a no-man's land hideous with rolls of barbed wire and concrete vehicle traps like obscenely oversized toys: land that grows nothing but broken glass and cinders and debris, and staring blindly down on it the faceless fronts of evacuated buildings no one tears down, with their empty windows of dirty and broken glass, or no glass at all, or, worst of all, bricked and plastered-over places three and four flights up where windows were eliminated because people jumped out and over the Wall — jumped and broke bones but unless fatally injured got out.

Each car going through has its gas tank checked for a live body concealed under a false bottom, the underneath of the car is examined with a mirror on a long rod for a person tied to the chassis. The watchtower at the center of the checkpoint has eyes and searchlights and guns. At night a person walks through, bathed in brilliance, aimed at from all directions with guns at the ready — any person, worrying about his old mother or difficult employer, nose dripping in the night air (and handkerchief in the other jacket), cocooned in his own little dwindling life. Important only to the few people he cares for, he suddenly becomes insanely important enough here to *shoot, dead* if he resides in the wrong place or has the wrong papers.

As if the walls inside myself, and yours in you, were not evil enough! As if it didn't take a lifetime of heartbreaking, humiliating, sometimes rewarded labor to blow them up and knock them down, or spirit them away. Maybe the inner walls we despise are what make this Wall so unspeakably intolerable, for here is a wall not to keep out marauders or armies, protect life from dangerous beasts or equinoctial tides, or even to safeguard property from theft and virgins from love, but to keep an ordinary guy (who needs to blow his nose) from visiting his sick mother and talking to a colleague about the boss over a couple of beers. A wall built for the sole and terrible purpose to divide, and division is of the devil.

We had wondered since our arrival where the fine old buildings were, and now, having crossed, we found out. They are all over there, the university and state library, the embassies and chancelleries, Unter den Linden itself, needing paint and repairs and care, decaying in the drabbest of settings. One vacant lot seemed not to have been touched since the 1945 bombing, the cathedral was a stack of charcoal, and everything looked as if seen through scratched and dirty glass. The people walking about among these dying wrecks looked well enough fed and dressed but they all seemed to walk quite slowly — not strolling for pleasure, either, just walking without purpose.

Our friend Heinrich Keilholz, designer of concert halls and acoustics doctor to ailing ones, had escorted us over in Felsenstein's car but was now obliged to leave us; the driver — a little round and shabbily dressed East Berliner (no West Berliner may drive across) — took us to the museum we wanted to visit, where he too left us. Down the center of the almost empty street, a double trolley car, denuded of paint, rocked squeakingly past. We had ten East German marks between us, and my long unused knowledge of the language. We felt very much alone.

The Pergamum Museum was another huge, grim-looking building, elephant-colored and dilapidated, built around a now weedy deserted court; no people in sight, no color, not a sign of life. A small dingy door in a corner of the courtyard appeared to be, and was, the only museum entrance. Inside there were some people about and a few attendants — elderly women in cotton housedresses, standing among the larger-than-life statuary and huge photographs of archaeological sites. We asked them for the Gates of Babylon (odd request!) and were waved on to where, from one room to the next, one passes from grayness and dust to walking between walls of such stunning color and brilliance and splendor the hair rose on my arms and I shuddered all over, as if a wind had risen. This was the great processional street of ancient Babylon; we were walking between walls of ceramic tile of intense lapis lazuli blue, walking between a double line of lions pacing along, teeth bared, tasseled tails streaming out behind — every detail exact down to the rise of the ankle which gives lions their gait of masterly ease. Not a tile broken or missing; the whole "street" gleaming, and at the end of it the Gate of Ishtar, its two towers sixty feet above us, of the same deep clear blue but decorated with proud bulls and an unknown mythological creature. Still farther on, the Pergamum Altar to Zeus, of still another kind of magnificence, with majesty of proportion and treasures of sculpture to haunt the mind's eye for life. What glory, what irony: these ancient, three-thousand-year-old celebrations in the middle of that graying wreckage of a generation ago; the brilliant ceremonial walls shut away behind that other evil Wall.

In the East Berlin waiting room at Checkpoint Charlie — tougher than the ingoing one — hung a sign with a quotation printed on it in large letters. Translated, this read:

> Great Carthage led three wars,
> It was still powerful after the first one,
> It was still inhabitable after the second;
> It no longer existed after the third.

The young man in uniform behind the counter who returned passports, examined each face and compared it with its photograph as if required to draw it from memory; the only part of his own face which ever moved was the eyes. *Ghastly!* I wanted to shout it.

There was nothing outwardly the matter with me when we were back in our room and dressing for the concert, but suddenly I couldn't face anything more. It was the only concert we had planned to attend, which we missed.

But we saw the other side of Berlin, too — the Berliners' gallantry and determination, the good-natured pluck with which they make the best of being imprisoned. For that is what they are: the Wall not only divides the city but completely surrounds it with its gray and barbed desert set with watchtowers. Given money enough, and valid reasons, Berliners may fly out (through those narrow corridors), take the train or even drive, through a hundred miles of Soviet-held land, but the process is made so difficult as to be a virtual deterrent. Jack Kirkman, even after an evening spent with a group of young Berliners, had trouble believing and absorbing what he learned from them. "Imagine," he said to me, "never being able just to drive out into the country on a weekend. They can go to one of the big city parks and walk in the woods, or row on a lake, but that's all. And the lakes are constantly patrolled by boats watching for swimmers with underwater gear . . . people have swum over, using snorkels."

Yet Berliners haven't lost the dry wit that has characterized them, while our own chief officials there were outstanding for their cheerfulness and their devotion to the brave citizens. Brewster Morris, head of the American Mission, and his wife gave Bernstein a small luncheon in the Mission residence — a comfortable and attractive house on a suburban street which might have been in Brookline or outside Philadelphia. It was a beautiful, highly civilized meal and occasion, made unforgettable by the people around the table: all of them — Mayor Schütz, our Commanding General Ferguson (who had lost his only son in Vietnam), Streseman (the *Intendant* of the Berlin Philharmonic), Hans Tuch, Morris's deputy, and their wives — all had a quality I can best convey as magnanimity and tolerance and goodwill.

The last night in Berlin brought also the last Mahler of the tour. It was the finest yet. How was it possible, I asked myself, after all the great performances it had been given, to sound still deeper, graver, and at the same time so shining? Did pity for the people of Berlin — and for all the imprisoned and brave everywhere — inspire that passion of tenderness? What was very clear, however, was that all the playing of it, and all the shared experiences of five weeks, had made of the musicians an instrument of such precision and flexibility they played with an almost superhuman unity — a fire flaming up at the faintest breath. At the end, there were tears on many faces, tears apparently of release and joy. A deep sense of gratitude and communion welled up in the audience; the walls were down.

"Mahler's Fifth unfolds like some huge and wonderful novel," Lenny once said. "It ought to be played without interruption — all by itself." Like other great works, one supposes it must continue to reveal itself to an interpreter equal to it, especially one for whom conducting is a process of discovery. I remember the televised interview in Amsterdam, how he had been questioned about his affinity for Mahler. The first part of his reply concerned the strange parallels, including mathematical coincidences, in their two lives (the fact that Mahler died at fifty, we thought, might account for some of his sadness this summer). "I don't really know why it is," he went on, "I can't explain it even to myself why Mahler means so much to me, but when I conduct him it is as if it were music I had written myself, was *in the process of composing*, so I feel as if I were improvising as I go along."

In improvisation — of any kind — duality, restraint, barriers dissolve; there is no music and musician, or movement and dancer, word and speaker; everything is one. Perhaps that was why, in that citadel of division, this example of the unity that is our home was so transcendent.

XIII

Cadenza

TOMMY JOINED US IN BERLIN — Tommy Thompson, Regional Editor of *Life* Magazine in Europe, sent to do an article on Bernstein. For the four days and nights of the tour that were left he shadowed Lenny everywhere, in conductors' dressing rooms, on flights, at meals, in cars, his tall stature and remarkably round head, the intensely blue and inquisitive eyes very much in evidence.

Tommy was recently back from Chicago, where he had been maced, though thanks to someone's quick action in dousing his eyes with water, he had soon recovered his sight. I asked him if he had been clubbed too, since he was one of the hundred or more people whom the police pushed against, and finally through, the plate-glass window of the hotel, beating them as they went. He answered in the most offhand way: of course; everyone was clubbed. Although he said it was no more than a glancing blow on the side of his neck, I noticed one hand go to his neck as he said it — memory became gesture.

"Now tell me," he asked (we were lunching together before

our trip to East Berlin), "what is there to be said about this man that hasn't been said before?"

I don't remember if I replied "Everything — and nothing," though it is certainly what I felt, words being about as effective at grasping such a personal and artistic phenomenon as the hand is at scooping up water. "That extraordinary creature," is how a mutual friend concludes any talk about him — an interesting noun, as if he were indeed created differently. Yet here is a man who is so open and direct one might say he is transparent, uninhibited, highly communicative. Why the problem? Is it just that everything about him is so much more so than in the rest of us? Or that his personality is so intense, his presence so vivid that one responds rather than being free to observe and describe? For it seems impossible for people to remain neutral toward him or unaffected by his presence; even at his most relaxed he gives out a sense of contained inner force, as if he really were differently animated from others — with more electricity, more connectedness, less resistance. (It was interesting to see on the tour that he never appeared to hurry; I don't believe I've ever seen him "in a hurry." His walk and speech are alike in their quiet authority and deliberateness; the speech measured, not because of uncertainty but because of giving himself room in which to pick the exact word or phrase — to be *in* what he's doing. Whether speaking or conducting, happily fooling, as at the Schloss, eating or walking through an airport, he commits himself totally to it — a perfect example of the Chinese sage's "When walking, just walk, when sitting, just sit, above all — don't wobble!" "The most with-it person I ever met," a young friend said, which, combined with the brilliant mind, can frighten less "with-it" people and scatter their wits.)

This kind of thing I felt sure Tommy would pick up at once, but what would he be able to see of Lenny as a whole, away from the family so deeply important to him, besieged by crowds and demands and unlikely in these last days to be in any natural setting? Quite a contrast to our own first meeting, ten years before, when he and Felicia and Marc Blitzstein came to see us in our remote house on Martha's Vineyard at the end of a web of rough and sandy little roads, overlooking the sea. They were late and we were beginning to suspect they were lost when we heard voices, first from one point in the dwarf oak woods, then, after car sounds and pauses, from somewhere else but chiefly one very resonant voice bursting out from time to time into huge laughter. We waited and listened, laughing ourselves, helpless; it was a scene right out of *A Midsummer Night's Dream* or *The Tempest*.

Sitting around in summer afternoon idleness, one of our family asked Lenny how he and Steve Sondheim had ever collaborated on the songs of *West Side Story*. How did collaboration work? This was 1958, a year after *West Side Story* opened; our own record of it was almost worn out. Lenny was about to be forty. Deeply tanned and dressed in casual summer clothes, he looked awfully young — no older than some of the cast — as he proceeded to describe his and Steve's torments and raptures of composition, to sing phrases of the music and act out parts of the show. It is the kind of thing at which he has excelled ever since summer vacations from high school when he did everything but write the Gilbert and Sullivan operettas produced with the neighbors in Sharon. (By one of life's curious coincidences the same small town outside Boston where my husband was born and where we lived when we were first married.) A few years later, before his Third Symphony, "Kaddish," had its United States premiere and he found the tape of its first performance in Israel was wrong for the machine at hand, he gave us a spellbinding one-man rendition of that: orchestral effects, narration, what the chorus was doing, stopping to explain the religious background and translate from the Hebrew as he went along.

Looking around our summer living room that afternoon, his eye was caught by a box of anagrams stuck high on a bookshelf — and we were for it. I came from a family who played word games with anyone they could cajole into joining them, but never have I lived through anything like the racing anagrams in which he at once had us all engaged, sitting around the dining room table in the August sun, frenziedly making and stealing words, crowing with triumph, groaning with despair. It was mad, and wonderful.

He was as interested as Felicia was in the house, which has many unusual features. How did I find it to live in, he asked me, was it glorious? The question happened to touch a nerve that still quivered from the prolonged pains of building, moving into an unfinished house, and learning new ways of living. I told him I was still finding out, and hadn't discovered yet how to entertain in it. "Does anyone know how to entertain?" he replied, and gave me a sympathetic smile. Then they left and we heard all over again as if in a *da capo al fine* the offstage car sounds on different curves and grades of the road, the voices diminishing with distance.

The memory is all there, held clear in the amber of midsummer. So much of him had been disclosed in a short time: the delight in acting and playing difficult games, the interest in everything around him, even (in his questioning me about the house) the uncanny instinct for sensing what is going on in someone else, an awareness of what the significant inner action is which feels like a separate sense. "Oh he knows *everything* that's going on in people," says one of his oldest friends. If it weren't for the wonderfully warm and loving nature — his loving-kindness, really — this might be highly disconcerting, and sometimes it is.

It was during the remaining summers the Bernsteins spent at the Vineyard, even more than in New York, that we came to know the man as well as the music-maker, and often during the tour, at the heart of the music, with him dancing it, pleading it out of the violins, jabbing at the percussion section, lashing and even clubbing it out of the air, I was struck by how inextricably they combine: the man and the music he makes, or, more accurately, the way he makes it. His communication of musical meaning to the orchestra and to his audiences, his eagerness to share this experience, seems the same that animates his own experiencing — not only of music but skiing or eating, swimming or playing with words or looking through binoculars at Jupiter's moons. He loses himself in the same way.

It is hardly surprising that with such deep feeling and immediate responsiveness he also moves from one emotion or state to another with startling rapidity. Almost as spontaneous as a child, he likes to live with as few constrictions as possible, abhorring any more planning ahead than absolutely necessary, leaving leeway for the unexpected. "Let's wing it" was a favorite reply on the tour to setting up in advance what might not fit when the time came. This spontaneity must be the delight and also the despair of his family; it certainly has been of tour managers. On an American tour, once, he and Carlos Moseley were on their way to the hall for the concert — well ahead of schedule, since the traffic (because of him) was dreadful — when he noticed they were passing an amusement park. Nothing could dissuade him from having a couple of rides on the roller coaster, "one of the biggest and worst in the whole country!" said Carlos with amused horror, "and nothing would stop him from eating a hot dog and some of that pink sugar fuzz first, and making me eat it with him." An irresponsible escapade, from which they arrived at the hall in the nick of time, one refreshed and the other a nervous wreck, yet one wonders if without that side of his nature too the music would sound as it does.

For it is a complex nature, full of apparently contradictory qualities. An enjoyer of life, almost a sensualist, one thinks, seeing how much he lives through the senses; a disciplined intellectual, one knows from listening to the explorations of his mind and the precision of language kept honed by those puzzles and games he tackles partly out of a fear that his mind might "grow fat." Behind every appearance a great intelligence is at work.

A very free spirit, he seems, until one discovers the New England puritanism, and a strong Hebrew sense of guilt as well; someone tuned to the future yet vibrating strongly to tradition. A man who, among his friends at two or three in the morning, sits at the piano and bawls out one popular song after another or goes the rounds of the discothèques, yet who basically stands close to the tragedy of existence and to human suffering, as we had seen in one country after another where hate, violence, refugees, injustice, imprisonment — all the faces of war — went by in dreadful procession. As long ago as Japan he had passionately burst out one evening with "*No more war!* There just can't be wars, anymore! Everyone in the world should have another language besides his own and if only everyone had the same 'other language' then we could all *communicate* with each other." Seven years older and with humanity's predicaments intensifying and proliferating at the same speed as its population, he was even more concerned, walking onstage to conduct Papa Haydn that night in Vienna so heartbroken he didn't know how he'd go through with it.

Only in the Vienna woods and that middle-of-the-night gambol had we seen on the tour his love of nature — of submerging himself in it, or else of studying with fascination a single small example of its marvels. Hearing him discuss scientific theories, seeing him contemplate for minutes on end a remarkably patterned feather, wondering aloud how the genes knew to put a dot here, that design there, one speculates on the scientist he might have been, but then, handing the feather over, "It's like one of Beethoven's last quartets" is what he says. First and last, music is the key; music is the driving force, the order that holds all in balance; music governs him and is what he governs.

Tommy would have the music in its climactic last concerts — particularly those concerts in Berlin, which of all the cities we had visited set Bernstein off the most vividly. There, too, his Jewishness seemed more Jewish and his feeling for people more intense and tender. The Berliners are also a persecuted people; he was the persecuted and the comforter both. To someone hearing and watching him there for the first time (as Tommy was) it was clearer than ever how his love for people — his musicians and audiences, the composers he plays, young people — is the fire at the center of the Bernstein phenomenon which, in combination with his talents, gives us music on a scale and in a way that are quite unfamiliar. Is it that love, too, which is behind the passion to share his own musical experience?

Critics have remarked that he is a born teacher who would like to make the whole world his classroom but that not every-

We live by intimations of what is,
So well the miracle we're part of keeps
Its secrets, so delicate its clues: a leaf
To tell the wind; a shell, the blood's tide —
Shadows on cave walls, just as Plato said.
Yet *something* outside the borders of ourselves
Moves, free, in the sun; the air quivers
With the invisible and the unheard.

It is the artist brings us near and nearer
Whatever lies beyond what's imaged, written,
Hacked out, played: art is the last high land
Breasting an ocean — a continent lies behind.
We can no more conceive that spacious grandeur
Than, deaf and blind, imagine the Pacific
But sometimes there's an artist who bears witness
Like those surf-shaken and sky-shrugging cliffs

Fog alternately blinds and leaves to stare
Across half the earth, who interprets the sea wind
As outmost cypresses assume its shape,
Conveys its rhythms like the wave-swung kelp;
Human, is of the land and seer, land's end
And being explorer, too, must stand and tell
What cliff cannot, must share discovery
With all of us, taking us by the hand,
Crying out: Come with me, look! The sea! The sea!

XIV

Coda

TWO CITIES, TWO CONCERTS, fifty-eight hours left after our lift-off out of Berlin; in Copenhagen it wasn't even twenty-four hours from landing to leaving. Copenhagen and London were almost home.

An hour after we had left gray Berlin we were drifting down over the thatched and red-tiled roofs of Danish farmhouses, over sunny fields dotted with cattle and the blue sound check-marked with white sails. The plane door was opened and we walked out into free air; the air of a free country snapped and rippled the many airport flags. There was an almost forgotten ease in the manner of the agent who escorted us from the plane, some distance out from the terminal, and if I remember only vaguely the vehicle that conveyed us there it is because of the young woman who drove it. Looking over her shoulder with an "Are we all ready, then?" she flashed a smile and drove away with us; in her look and manner, as in that of the agent's, lay a world of difference from the storm centers left behind. It came from more than individual temperament, I feel sure, but from what, exactly? There was great naturalness and confidence in it, but again, why? What common assumption underlay it, what assurance that all was well between us? I like you, it said; we can be friends. And more even than "I know you are people of goodwill who won't do harm — I trust you," I think perhaps it said, from unconscious depths, "I can endure harm — my ancestors and many of my countrymen have done so; and this little land I live in, though it was powerful once and conquered and ruled Sweden and Norway, has no power now. I can endure harm but I won't inflict it; there is nothing to inflict it with. So I am free to greet you, and make friends."

The small bus (or whatever it was) rolled to a stop outside an entrance, flags tickled the blue air overhead, and the girl jumped down. The tissue of faith, gashed and shredded in so many places, was once more whole.

In the terminal proper, musicians from the Danish Symphony stood gathered and at Bernstein's appearance broke into a passage from the Witches' Sabbath of the *Fantastique*, at which he and his musicians burst out laughing. Everyone seemed very gay and relaxed, and until we left next morning we were to keep hearing, as we heard in Amsterdam, "If only we could stay!"

Copenhagen's adoration of Bernstein was rather like Vienna's, and here too, though he had conducted (and been awarded the Sonning Prize for great achievement), he was coming for the first time with his own orchestra. He needed protecting, particularly from a reporter and photographer assigned to do a feature article on "Twenty-four Hours with Bernstein" who scarcely left him alone. He seemed dreadfully tired, the reporter observed to me. "He is," I told her. "Berlin, with three straight concerts was particularly hard —

Germany was hard." She said nothing but threw me a sharp look.

I cannot write with detachment of the concert there, or the acclaim, or the party afterwards in our embassy residence out in the suburbs: it was all too much home — my mother's city and country where I have visited since I was a child (and have written of elsewhere), with relatives in that audience whom I had less chance to see than many strangers in other cities. Once, after leaving Copenhagen as a young girl when I had just spent two of the happiest weeks of my life, I dreamed and had fantasies for months of suddenly reappearing there — being magically set down in streets I knew and walking in on people I loved, perhaps surprising them at table and joining them for one of those meals Danes know so well how to turn into a celebration — and here, all these years later it was happening: fantasy made fact, though too briefly really to savor, too long afterwards for many people still to be living and the family meal stretched to include two hundred, yet managing even so to have that Danish sense of coziness and informality somehow mixed with ceremony.

It was all a homecoming. It had over it, as Denmark always has for me, a kind of bright innocence a little too good to believe. Which it almost was . . . When we arrived at and left the embassy residence, the front door was unlocked for us and quickly locked again; someone murmured an embarrassed explanation: there had been threats of an anti-American, anti-Vietnam war demonstration. Driving back into town along the shore road, Strandvejen, past dark beech forests and the little lights of yacht basins where hundreds of sailboats and small yachts lay bridled bow and stern, waiting for their owners to come on bicycles and take the family out for a weekend sail, Lenny said very quietly, "Denmark is somehow out of the Great World, yet free; the opposite of Berlin." But, a moment later: could it last? would anything of the civilization we knew survive?

No one wanted to leave, yet when we arrived in London, which was so much more familiar, and slipped into our own language again it was even nearer home. You could almost feel us settle down — migrant birds coming in to a pond at dusk. You could feel, too, the end-of-journey wistfulness: the last concert; the last night on that side of the ocean; the last night all together. We had come through so much, shared so deeply, companioned the whole way not only by each other but also by those opposites between which we kept being swung as if between the poles: conflict and concert, violence and peace, division and unity. The closer together they came, those swings, the nearer to one another those countries with their sharp differences, the more extreme the need and craving for that other world of music, world without walls. No other art is so uniting, nor such food. Painting, sculpture, literature, architecture call up the critic in us; music, though of the intellect too, is of the senses and emotions, affects pulse and breath, brings shivers and tears, stirs the unconscious like dreams and myth.

Although some of the English music critics (alone among all those who reviewed the tour's twenty-four concerts) were critical of Bernstein and his orchestra, the audience responded and demonstrated about as wildly as anywhere else. It was a last Berlioz for us — and the first commercially televised classical concert England had ever had. The young man who dressed my hair a few days later and had watched it said, "It was *superb.* I was just riveted to the set, and I don't like classical music — can't bear it usually. But Bernstein, he *becomes* every instrument in the orchestra, you feel him draw it out of them; even if they weren't good musicians he'd get good music from them. And the musicians' faces! You could see their love for him — every one." I asked him how he happened to turn to that channel if he didn't like music. Out of curiosity, he said; thought he'd watch five minutes but couldn't turn to another channel, although football was his favorite and halfway through the *Fantastique* there was a football match on another channel. "My wife couldn't get over it," he finished, "me missing my football."

My goal is communicating . . . the one language we all have in common. The mind talks in a babel of languages, each mind chattering endlessly away to itself, different minds having endless trouble in communicating; even lovers, when they use words, misunderstand one another. In music, as in making love, mind follows or accompanies, is neither oppressive nor oppressed, moves in perfect ease and grace.

After the last Berlioz and a last huge reception in Festival Hall came the day of return. The tour was over. I was not flying home with the rest and was to suffer from this, thoughts and feelings stretched to their utmost trying to follow where I felt I belonged. With no daily concerts and the music-makers gone, the air would feel dead and still, London have the ocean's empty roar.

At noon on the day of departure, Jack let me into Bernstein's suite to say goodbye. In the darkened living room ten people must have been gathered; he had just finished auditioning a young mezzo-soprano. She stood beside the piano, while agents, managers, all the others were scattered around the room and Bernstein was telling her in a kind and serious tone how important it was for her to keep to the repertoire for which the special quality of her voice was suited. The moment he finished, people moved forward around him. It was the usual Mr. Bernstein . . . Lenny, when you're through . . . Chaplin called, he'll be here at four . . . Here's a message from . . . It was only a few hours since he had gone to bed; it was to be at least eighteen hours more before he would land in New York. Did he *ever* have five minutes' privacy? I asked him. Almost never, he smiled — and admired the fabric of the dress I was wearing.

Jack and I went into another room, where I said goodbye to Tommy; he had been up most of the night talking with "his man" and now had that look of dazed and childlike submission people get when they pass a certain point of fatigue. Behind him, shining through the gently blowing curtains, the river was moving majestically past Festival Hall, around the curve and away under Waterloo Bridge.

Jack stood in the doorway, his eyes unusually dark in his face, all the brightness gone out of them. I told him I'd see him back in New York again soon — at the concert, not next week, but the week after that.

His reply still sounds somewhere, in the mind's ear, like a cry: "But it will never be the same again!"

And of course he was right. How could it be?

SECOND VIOLINS

Leopold Rybb
Oscar Weizner
Eugene Bergen
Luigi Carlini
Nathan Goldstein
Martin Eshelman
Carlos Piantini
Bernard Robbins
Theodor Podnos
Allan Schiller
W. Sanford Allen
Oscar Ravina
Michael de Stefano
Richard Simon
Gino Sambuco

VIOLAS

William Lincer
Leonard Davis
Sol Greitzer
Ralph Mendelson
Selig Posner
Eugene Becker
Henry Nigrine
Larry Newland
William Carboni
Raymond Sabinsky
Harry G. Zaratzian
Erich Silberstein

CELLOS

Lorne Munroe
Nathan Stutch
Gerald K. Appleman
George Feher
Lorin Bernsohn
Paul Clement
Avram Lavin
Jurgen DeLemos
Thomas Liberti
Asher Richman
Mrs. Evangeline Benedetti
Martin Ormandy

BASSES

Robert Brennand
John Schaeffer
Walter Botti
Homer Mensch
Miss Orin O'Brien
James Candido
Lew Norton
Alvin Brehm
David Walter

FLUTES

Julius Baker
Robert Morris
Paige Brook

New York Philharmonic

Tour of Europe and Israel, 1968

TOUR PERSONNEL

Leonard Bernstein, Conductor
Alain Lombard, Associate Tour Conductor

Orchestra

FIRST VIOLINS

David Nadien,
Concertmaster
Frank Gullino,
Assistant Concertmaster
Joseph Bernstein,
2nd Assistant Concertmaster
William Dembinsky
Bjoern Andreasson
Alfio Micci
Leon Temerson
Kenneth Gordon
Max Weiner
Leon Rudin
Carlo Renzulli
William Nowinski
Louis Fishzohn
Morris Borodkin
Newton Mansfield
Enrico DiCecco
Joachim Fishberg
Mrs. Joyce Flissler Mendelson

PICCOLO

F. William Heim

OBOES

Harold Gomberg
Jerome Roth
Albert Goltzer

ENGLISH HORN

Engelbert Brenner

CLARINETS

Stanley Drucker
Michael Burgio

E-FLAT CLARINET

Peter Simenauer

BASS CLARINET

Stephen Freeman

BASSOONS

Manuel Zegler
Frank Ruggieri
Harold Goltzer

CONTRABASSOON

Bert Bial

HORNS

Joseph Singer
Ranier De Intinis
A. Robert Johnson
John Carabella
William Namen
Fred Klein
John Wunderlich
Ezra Molcho

TRUMPETS

William Vacchiano
Carmine Fornarotto
John Ware
James Smith
Albert Ligotti

TROMBONES

Edward Herman, Jr.
Gilbert Cohen
Allen Ostrander
Edward Erwin

TUBA

Joseph Novotny

TIMPANI

Saul Goodman

PERCUSSION

Walter Rosenberger
Elden Bailey
Morris Lang

HARP

Myor Rosen
Mrs. Phyllis Wright

ORCHESTRA PERSONNEL MANAGER

Joseph De Angelis

ASSISTANT PERSONNEL MANAGER

John A. Schaeffer

LIBRARIAN

Howard Keresey

ASSISTANT LIBRARIAN

* Joseph Zizza

STAGE REPRESENTATIVE

Francis Nelson

ASSISTANT STAGE REPRESENTATIVES

Peter Regan Robert Hart
Edouard Ebner

Administration

William Weissel, Assistant Manager
Albert K. Webster, Assistant Manager
Frank W. Milburn, Press Director and Music Administrator
Kenneth Haas, Assistant to the Managing Director
Alice de Berry, Executive Secretary
Anatole Heller, Agent

* Deceased

Also Accompanying Tour

Dr. Paul Zea, Physician
Jack Kirkman, Valet to Mr. Bernstein

Members of the Philharmonic
Who Were Unable to Go on the Tour

Bernardo Altmann, cello
James Chambers, horn
Mordecai Dayan, violin
David Kates, viola
Jacques Margolies, violin
Mario Polisi, bass
Benjamin Schlossberg, bass
Robert Weinrebe, viola

Carlos D. Moseley, Managing Director